PRACTICE - ASSESS - D

180 Days of LANGUAGE
for Kindergarten

✓ capitalization
✓ punctuation
✓ parts of speech
✓ spelling

Author
Christine Dugan, M.A.Ed.

SHELL EDUCATION

Image Credits

All images Shutterstock

Standards

Shell Education

5301 Oceanus Drive

Huntington Beach, CA 92649-1030

http://www.shelleducation.com

ISBN 978-1-4258-1172-3

© 2015 Shell Education Publishing, Inc.

TABLE OF CONTENTS

INTRODUCTION AND RESEARCH

People who love the English language often lament the loss of grammar knowledge and the disappearance of systematic grammar instruction. We wince at emails with errors, such as when the noun *advice* is used instead of the verb *advise* is required. We may set aside a résumé with the incorrect placement of an apostrophe. And some of us pore (not pour) over entertaining punctuation guides such as *Eats, Shoots and Leaves* by Lynne Truss (2003). We chuckle over collections of bloopers such as *Anguished English: An Anthology of Accidental Assaults upon Our Language* by Richard Lederer (1987).

Even though we worry about grammar, our students arrive at school with a complex set of grammar rules in place—albeit affected by the prevailing dialect (Hillocks and Smith 2003, 727). For example, while students may not be able to recite the rule for where to position an adjective, they know intuitively to say *the yellow flower* instead of *the flower yellow*. All this knowledge comes without formal instruction. Further, young people easily shift between articulating or writing traditional patterns of grammar and communicating complete sentences with startling efficiency: IDK (I don't know), and for the ultimate in brevity, K (okay).

So, if students speak fairly well and have already mastered a complex written shorthand, why study grammar? Researchers provide us with three sound reasons:

1. the insights it offers into the way the language works

2. its usefulness in mastering standard forms of English

3. its usefulness in improving composition skills (Hillocks and Smith 1991, 594)

INTRODUCTION AND RESEARCH *(cont.)*

Studying grammar also provides users—teachers, students, and parents—with a common vocabulary to discuss both spoken and written language. The Assembly for the Teaching of English Grammar states, "Grammar is important because it is the language that makes it possible for us to talk about language. Grammar names the types of words and word groups that make up sentences not only in English but in any language. As human beings, we can put sentences together even as children—we all *do* grammar. But to be able to talk about how sentences are built, about the types of words and word groups that make up sentences—that is *knowing about* grammar."

With the publication of the Common Core State Standards, key instructional skills are identified, such as identifying parts of speech, using prepositional phrases, capitalization, and correctly using commas. Writing conventions such as punctuation serve an important function for the reader— setting off syntactic units and providing intonational cues and semantic information. Capitalization provides the reader with such cues as sentence beginnings and proper nouns (Hodges 1991, 779).

The Need for Practice

To be successful in today's classroom, students must deeply understand both concepts and procedures so that they can discuss and demonstrate their understanding. Demonstrating understanding is a process that must be continually practiced in order for students to be successful. According to Marzano, "practice has always been, and always will be, a necessary ingredient to learning procedural knowledge at a level at which students execute it independently" (2010, 83). Practice is especially important to help students apply their concrete, conceptual understanding of a particular language skill.

Understanding Assessment

In addition to providing opportunities for frequent practice, teachers must be able to assess students' comprehension and word-study skills. This is important so that teachers can adequately address students' misconceptions, build on their current understanding, and challenge them appropriately. Assessment is a long-term process that often involves careful analysis of student responses from a lesson discussion, project, practice sheet, or test. When analyzing the data, it is important for teachers to reflect on how their teaching practices may have influenced students' responses, and to identify those areas where additional instruction may be required. In short, the data gathered from assessments should be used to inform instruction: slow down, speed up, or reteach. This type of assessment is called *formative assessment.*

HOW TO USE THIS BOOK

With *180 Days of Language,* students receive practice with punctuation, identifying parts of speech, capitalization, and spelling. The daily practice will develop students' writing efforts and oral reading skills.

Easy to Use and Standards-Based

These activities reinforce grade-level skills across a variety of language concepts. The questions are provided as a full practice page, making them easy to prepare and implement as part of a classroom morning routine, at the beginning of each language arts lesson, or as homework.

Every practice page provides questions that are tied to a language standard. Students are given opportunities for regular practice in language skills, allowing them to build confidence through these quick standards-based activities.

Question	Language Skill	Common Core State Standard
1	capitalization	**Language.K.2.a**—Capitalize the first word in a sentence and the pronoun *I*.
2	punctuation	**Language.K.2.a**—Recognize and name end punctuation.
3	parts of speech	**Language.K.1.b**—Use frequently occurring nouns and verbs. **Language.K.1.c**—Form regular plural nouns orally by adding /s/ or /es/ (e.g., dog, dogs; wish, wishes).
4	spelling	**Language.K.2.d**—Spell simple words phonetically, drawing on knowledge of sound-letter relationships.

HOW TO USE THIS BOOK *(cont.)*

Using the Practice Pages

Practice pages provide instruction and assessment opportunities for each day of the school year. Teachers may wish to prepare packets of weekly practice pages for the classroom or for homework. As outlined on page 5, every question is aligned to a language skill.

Practice pages provide instruction and assessment opportunities for each day of the school year.

Each question ties student practice to a specific language skill.

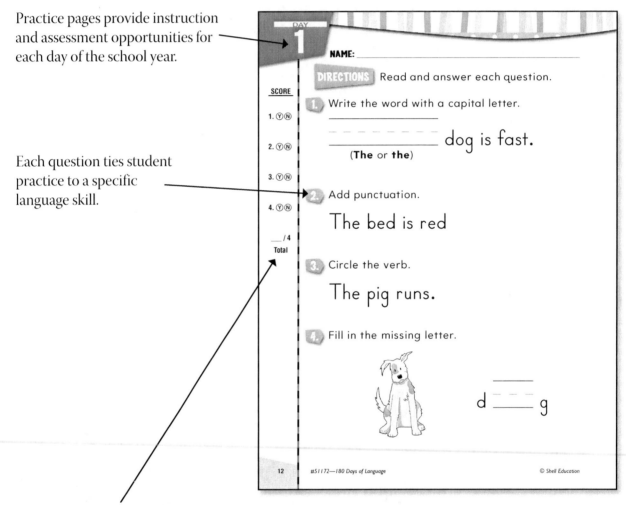

Using the Scoring Guide

Use the scoring guide along the side of each practice page to check answers and see at a glance which skills may need more reinforcement.

Fill in the appropriate circle for each problem to indicate correct (Y) or incorrect (N) responses. You might wish to indicate only incorrect responses to focus on those skills. (For example, if students consistently miss items 2 and 4, they may need additional help with those concepts as outlined in the table on page 5.) Use the answer key at the back of the book to score the problems, or you may call out answers to have students self-score or peer-score their work.

HOW TO USE THIS BOOK *(cont.)*

Diagnostic Assessment

Teachers can use the practice pages as diagnostic assessments. The data analysis tools included with the book enable teachers or parents to quickly score students' work and monitor their progress. Teachers and parents can see at a glance which language skills students may need to target in order to develop proficiency.

After students complete a practice page, grade each page using the answer key (pages 192–199). Then, complete the *Practice Page Item Analysis* for the appropriate day (page 8) for the whole class, or the *Student Item Analysis* (page 9) for individual students. These charts are also provided on the Digital Resource CD as PDFs, Microsoft Word® files, and as Microsoft Excel® files (filenames: pageitem.pdf, pageitem.doc, pageitem.xls; studentitem.pdf, studentitem.doc, studentitem.xls). Teachers can input data into the electronic files directly on the computer, or they can print the pages and analyze students' work using paper and pencil.

To complete the Practice Page Item Analyses:

- Write or type students' names in the far-left column. Depending on the number of students, more than one copy of the form may be needed, or you may need to add rows.

- The item numbers are included across the top of the chart. Each item correlates with the matching question number from the practice page.

- For each student, record an *X* in the column if the student has the item incorrect. If the item is correct, leave the space in the column blank.

- If you are using the Excel file, totals will be automatically generated. If you are using the Word file or if you have printed the PDF, you will need to compute the totals. Count the *X*s in each row and column and fill in the correct boxes.

To complete the Student Item Analyses:

- Write or type the student's name on the top row. This form tracks the ongoing progress of each student, so one copy per student is necessary.

- The item numbers are included across the top of the chart. Each item correlates with the matching question number from the practice page.

- For each day, record an *X* in the column if the student has the item incorrect. If the item is correct, leave the space in the column blank.

- If you are using the Excel file, totals will be automatically generated. If you are using the Word file or if you have printed the PDF, you will need to compute the totals. Count the *X*s in each row and column and fill in the correct boxes.

HOW TO USE THIS BOOK *(cont.)*

Practice Page Item Analysis

Directions: Record an *X* in cells to indicate where students have missed questions. Add up the totals. You can view: (1) which questions/concepts were missed per student; (2) the total correct score for each student; and (3) the total number of students who missed each question.

Day: _____ Question # Student Name	1	2	3	4	# correct
Sample Student		x			3/4
# of students missing each question					

HOW TO USE THIS BOOK (cont.)

Student Item Analysis

Directions: Record an *X* in cells to indicate where the student has missed questions. Add up the totals. You can view: (1) which questions/concepts the student missed; (2) the total correct score per day; and (3) the total number of times each question/concept was missed.

Student Name: Sample Student					
Question	**1**	**2**	**3**	**4**	**# correct**
Day					
1		X			3/4
Total					

HOW TO USE THIS BOOK *(cont.)*

Using the Results to Differentiate Instruction

Once results are gathered and analyzed, teachers can use the results to inform the way they differentiate instruction. The data can help determine which concepts are the most difficult for students and which need additional instructional support and continued practice. Depending on how often the practice pages are scored, results can be considered for instructional support on a daily or weekly basis.

Whole-Class Support

The results of the diagnostic analysis may show that the entire class is struggling with a particular concept or group of concepts. If these concepts have been taught in the past, this indicates that further instruction or reteaching is necessary. If these concepts have not been taught in the past, this data is a great preassessment and may demonstrate that students do not have a working knowledge of the concepts. Thus, careful planning for the length of the unit(s) or lesson(s) must be considered, and additional front-loading may be required.

Small-Group or Individual Support

The results of the diagnostic analysis may show that an individual or a small group of students is struggling with a particular concept or group of concepts. If these concepts have been taught in the past, this indicates that further instruction or reteaching is necessary. Consider pulling aside these students while others are working independently to instruct further on the concept(s). Teachers can also use the results to help identify individuals or groups of proficient students who are ready for enrichment or above-grade-level instruction. These students may benefit from independent learning contracts or more challenging activities. Students may also benefit from extra practice using games or computer-based resources.

My Language Book

Make copies of the *My Language Book* (pages 200–206) for students. Depending on students' abilities, have them reference this book while working on the activity pages.

Digital Resource CD

The Digital Resource CD provides all of the activity pages and all of the diagnostic pages in this book. The list of resources on the CD can be found on page 208.

STANDARDS CORRELATIONS

Shell Education is committed to producing educational materials that are research and standards based. In this effort, we have correlated all of our products to the academic standards of all 50 states, the District of Columbia, the Department of Defense Dependents Schools, and all Canadian provinces.

How to Find Standards Correlations

To print a customized correlation report of this product for your state, visit our website at http://www.shelleducation.com and follow the on-screen directions. If you require assistance in printing correlation reports, please contact our Customer Service Department at 1-877-777-3450.

Purpose and Intent of Standards

Legislation mandates that all states adopt academic standards that identify the skills students will learn in kindergarten through grade twelve. Many states also have standards for Pre–K. This same legislation sets requirements to ensure the standards are detailed and comprehensive.

Standards are designed to focus instruction and guide adoption of curricula. Standards are statements that describe the criteria necessary for students to meet specific academic goals. They define the knowledge, skills, and content students should acquire at each level. Standards are also used to develop standardized tests to evaluate students' academic progress. Teachers are required to demonstrate how their lessons meet state standards. State standards are used in the development of all of our products, so educators can be assured they meet the academic requirements of each state.

Common Core State Standards

The activities in this book are aligned to the Common Core State Standards (CCSS). The chart on page 5 lists the standards. The chart is also on the Digital Resource CD (filename: standards.pdf).

NAME: _____

SCORE

1. Ⓨ Ⓝ

2. Ⓨ Ⓝ

3. Ⓨ Ⓝ

4. Ⓨ Ⓝ

___ / 4
Total

DIRECTIONS Read and answer each question.

1. Write the word with a capital letter.

_____

_ _ _ _ _ _ _ _ _ _ dog is fast.
_____
(The or **the)**

2. Add punctuation.

The bed is red

3. Circle the verb.

The pig runs.

4. Fill in the missing letter.

d _ _ _ _ g

NAME: _____

DIRECTIONS Read and answer each question.

1. Write the word with a capital letter.

_____

_ _ _
_____ pan is hot.
(**a** or **A**)

2. Add punctuation.

A boy is in the car

3. Circle the plural noun.

cat   cats

4. Fill in the missing letter.

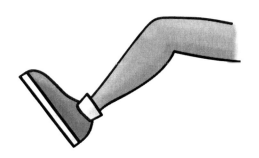

_ _ _
l _ _ _ g

NAME: _____

DIRECTIONS Read and answer each question.

1. Write the word with a capital letter.

_____

_ _ _ _ _ _ _
_____ go to bed.

(**we** or **We**)

2. Add punctuation.

Is that a pet

3. Circle the noun.

The boy digs.

4. Fill in the missing letter.

b _ _ _ t

 #51172—180 Days of Language

NAME: _____

Read and answer each question.

1. Write the word with a capital letter.

_____

_____ is my mom.
(**She** or **she**)

2. Add punctuation.

Why did you go

3. Circle the plural noun.

hat   hats

4. Fill in the missing letter.

r _____ t

SCORE

1. Ⓨ Ⓝ

2. Ⓨ Ⓝ

3. Ⓨ Ⓝ

4. Ⓨ Ⓝ

___ / 4
Total

NAME: _____

DIRECTIONS Read and answer each question.

1. Write the word with a capital letter.

_____

_ _ _ _ _ _ _ _ _ _ is home?
_____
(**who** or **Who**)

2. Add punctuation.

The jet is loud

3. Circle the plural noun.

toe   toes

4. Fill in the missing letter.

t _ _ y

NAME: _____

DIRECTIONS Read and answer each question.

1. Write the word with a capital letter.

_____

_____ cat is fat.

(**the** or **The**)

2. Add punctuation.

The cat is sad

3. Circle the plural noun.

mom   moms

4. Fill in the missing letter.

h ___ n

NAME: _____

DIRECTIONS Read and answer each question.

1. Write the word with a capital letter.

_____

‾ ‾ ‾
_____ rat is wet.
(**A** or **a**)

2. Add punctuation.

When do we go

3. Circle the verb.

The top spins.

4. Fill in the missing letter.

m ‾‾‾ d

NAME: _____

DIRECTIONS Read and answer each question.

1. Write the word with a capital letter.

_____

_ _ _ _ _ _ _ _ _ boy is sad.
_____
(**The** or **the**)

1. Ⓨ Ⓝ

2. Ⓨ Ⓝ

2. Add punctuation.

I am very sad

3. Ⓨ Ⓝ

4. Ⓨ Ⓝ

___ / 4
Total

3. Circle the plural noun.

lid   lids

4. Fill in the missing letter.

b ___ g

NAME: _____

Read and answer each question.

SCORE

1. Ⓨ Ⓝ

2. Ⓨ Ⓝ

3. Ⓨ Ⓝ

4. Ⓨ Ⓝ

___ / 4
Total

1. Write the word with a capital letter.

_____

_____ the bug run?

(**will** or **Will**)

2. Add punctuation.

I love to read

3. Circle the verb.

The boy hugs me.

4. Fill in the missing letter.

c ____ p

 #51172—180 Days of Language

NAME: _____

DIRECTIONS Read and answer each question.

SCORE

1. Ⓨ Ⓝ

2. Ⓨ Ⓝ

3. Ⓨ Ⓝ

4. Ⓨ Ⓝ

___ / 4
Total

1. Write the word with a capital letter.

_____

_____ you go?

(**can** or **Can**)

2. Add punctuation.

I will eat now

3. Write the verb.

_____

The cat _____.

(**hops** or **red**)

4. Fill in the missing letter.

p ___ t

NAME: _____

1. Ⓨ Ⓝ

2. Ⓨ Ⓝ

3. Ⓨ Ⓝ

4. Ⓨ Ⓝ

___ / 4
Total

DIRECTIONS Read and answer each question.

1. Write the word with a capital letter.

_____

_ _ _ _ _ _ _ _ _ I go?
_____
(**can** or **Can**)

2. Add punctuation.

The tent is wet

3. Circle the plural noun.

mop   mops

4. Fill in the missing letter.

c _ _ _ _ t

NAME: _____

DIRECTIONS Read and answer each question.

1. Write the word with a capital letter.

_____

_ _ _ _ _ _ _ _ you hop?
_____
(**Do** or **do**)

2. Add punctuation.

Who will win

3. Write the verb.

The bug _____.
_ _ _ _ _ _ _ _
(**rug** or **ran**)

4. Fill in the missing letter.

pe _ _ _

NAME: _____

DIRECTIONS Read and answer each question.

1. Write the word with a capital letter.

_____

_ _ _ _ _ _ _ _ _ _ _ _ I be late?
_____
(will or **Will)**

2. Add punctuation.

She is very happy

3. Circle the noun.

The pot is hot.

4. Fill in the missing letter.

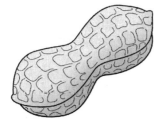

_____
_ _ _ _ _ _ ut

NAME: _____

Read and answer each question.

1. Write the word with a capital letter.

_____

_ _ _ _ _ dad can jog.

(**a** or **A**)

2. Add punctuation.

I have a cut

3. Circle the noun.

The lamp is red.

4. Fill in the missing letter.

h _ _ _ t

NAME: _____

DIRECTIONS Read and answer each question.

1. Write the word with a capital letter.

_____

_ _ _ _ _ _ _ _ I see?
_____
(can or **Can)**

2. Add punctuation.

Max is ten

3. Circle the verb.

The dog runs.

4. Fill in the missing letter.

si _ _ _ _

NAME: _____

DIRECTIONS Read and answer each question.

1. Write the word with a capital letter.

_____

_ _ _ _
_____ have a dog.
(i)

2. Add punctuation.

I like the pink cap

3. Circle the verb.

Mom led me home.

4. Fill in the missing letter.

_____
_ _ _
_____ og

SCORE

1. Ⓨ Ⓝ

2. Ⓨ Ⓝ

3. Ⓨ Ⓝ

4. Ⓨ Ⓝ

___ / 4
Total

NAME: _____

DIRECTIONS Read and answer each question.

1. Write the word with a capital letter.

_____

_____ cat is black.
(my)

2. Add punctuation.

That bump is big

3. Circle the verb.

Can you jog?

4. Fill in the missing letter.

v ___ t

NAME: _____

DIRECTIONS Read and answer each question.

1. Write the word with a capital letter.

_____

_ _ _ _
_____ can run.
(i)

2. Add punctuation.

Who can mop

3. Circle the noun.

She wants a toy.

4. Fill in the missing letter.

m _____ p

SCORE

1. Ⓨ Ⓝ

2. Ⓨ Ⓝ

3. Ⓨ Ⓝ

4. Ⓨ Ⓝ

___ / 4
Total

NAME: _____

DIRECTIONS Read and answer each question.

SCORE

1. Ⓨ Ⓝ

2. Ⓨ Ⓝ

3. Ⓨ Ⓝ

4. Ⓨ Ⓝ

___ / 4
Total

1. Write the word with a capital letter.

_____

_ _ _ _ _ _ _ _ _

_____ you go, too?
(**did**)

2. Add punctuation.

Will you get me

3. Circle the plural noun.

pin   pins

4. Fill in the missing letter.

10   t ___ n

NAME: _____

DIRECTIONS Read and answer each question.

1. Write the word with a capital letter.

The dog and ___ will run.
(i)

2. Add punctuation.

The pot is very hot

3. Circle the plural noun.

mat   mats

4. Fill in the missing letter.

f ___ n

NAME: _____

SCORE

DIRECTIONS Read and answer each question.

1. (Y)(N)

1. Write the word with a capital letter.

_____

2. (Y)(N)

_ _ _ have a cut.
_____
(i)

3. (Y)(N)

2. Add punctuation.

4. (Y)(N)

Where do we go

___ / 4
Total

3. Write the noun.

_____

The _____ is red.
(**sock** or **skip**)

4. Fill in the missing letter.

d ___ d

#51172—180 Days of Language
© Shell Education

NAME: _____

DIRECTIONS Read and answer each question.

SCORE

1. Ⓨ Ⓝ

2. Ⓨ Ⓝ

3. Ⓨ Ⓝ

4. Ⓨ Ⓝ

___ / 4
Total

1. Write the word with a capital letter.

_____

‾ ‾ ‾ ‾ ‾ ‾
_____ mom ran.
(**the**)

2. Add punctuation.

When is it over

3. Write the noun.

_____

My ‾ ‾ ‾ ‾ ‾ ‾ is wet.
(**hair** or **hop**)

4. Fill in the missing letter.

p ‾ ‾ ‾ t

NAME: _____

DIRECTIONS Read and answer each question.

1. Write the word with a capital letter.

_____

_ _ _ _____ cow can sit.
      (a)

2. Add punctuation.

I did that for you

3. Write the noun.

_____
The _____ sat on the rug.
   (red or **dog)**

4. Fill in the missing letter.

_____
d _____ g

NAME: _____

DIRECTIONS Read and answer each question.

1. Circle the word that needs a capital letter.

will he go, too?

2. Add punctuation.

The run is not fun

3. Circle the verb.

Jack hops on his foot.

4. Fill in the missing letter.

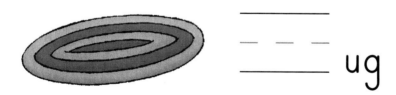 _____ ug

SCORE

1. Ⓨ Ⓝ

2. Ⓨ Ⓝ

3. Ⓨ Ⓝ

4. Ⓨ Ⓝ

___ / 4
Total

NAME: _____

DIRECTIONS Read and answer each question.

1. Circle the word that needs a capital letter.

do you see it?

2. Add punctuation.

The pen is blue

3. Circle the verb.

Anna runs away.

4. Fill in the missing letter.

h ___ t

NAME: _____

DIRECTIONS Read and answer each question.

1. Circle the word that needs a capital letter.

can I fit?

2. Add punctuation.

The lamp is off

3. Write the noun.

The _____ runs to me.

(**boy** or **hops**)

4. Fill in the missing letter.

_____ ug

NAME: _____

DIRECTIONS Read and answer each question.

1. Ⓨ Ⓝ

1. Circle the word that needs a capital letter.

is that a bad way to go?

2. Ⓨ Ⓝ

3. Ⓨ Ⓝ

2. Add punctuation.

The nest is on the tree

4. Ⓨ Ⓝ

___/ 4
Total

3. Write the verb.

The baby _____.

(**dad** or **naps**)

4. Fill in the missing letter.

c ____ p

#51172—180 Days of Language

NAME: _____

DIRECTIONS Read and answer each question.

1. Circle the word that needs a capital letter.

it is a big rig.

2. Add punctuation.

Who can help me

3. Write the noun.

The _____ can tap.
(**ran** or **man**)

4. Fill in the missing letter.

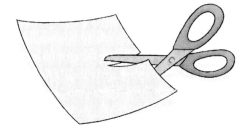

cu ____

SCORE

1. Ⓨ Ⓝ

2. Ⓨ Ⓝ

3. Ⓨ Ⓝ

4. Ⓨ Ⓝ

___ / 4
Total

NAME: _____

DIRECTIONS Read and answer each question.

1. Y N

2. Y N

3. Y N

4. Y N

___ / 4
Total

1. Circle the word that needs a capital letter.

the jug is pink.

2. Add punctuation.

Will you rest

3. Write the noun.

The _____ is on his head.
(**sat** or **cap**)

4. Fill in the missing letter.

p __ n

NAME: _____

DIRECTIONS   Read and answer each question.

1. Circle the word that needs a capital letter.

an apple is red.

2. Add punctuation.

That car is fast

3. Write the verb.

Mom will _____ it.
(**cat** or **fix**)

4. Fill in the missing letter.

_____
_ _ _ _
_____ us

NAME: _____

SCORE

1. (Y) (N)

2. (Y) (N)

3. (Y) (N)

4. (Y) (N)

___ / 4
Total

1. Write the word with a capital letter.

_____

_ _ _ _ dog rests.
(a)

2. Add punctuation.

The vest is wet

3. Write the noun.

_____

The _ _ _ _ _ _ _ _ _ is pink.
(**rose** or **fun**)

4. Fill in the missing letter.

_____

s _ _ _ d

NAME: _____

DIRECTIONS Read and answer each question.

1. Write the word with a capital letter.

_____

_ _ _ _ _ _ _ _ _ _ sand is hot.
(the)

2. Add punctuation.

Is that a big sink

3. Write the noun.

The _ _ _ _ _ _ _ _ _ is fast.
(lion or **cool)**

4. Fill in the missing letter.

j _ _ g

NAME: _____

DIRECTIONS Read and answer each question.

SCORE

1. Ⓨ Ⓝ

2. Ⓨ Ⓝ

3. Ⓨ Ⓝ

4. Ⓨ Ⓝ

___ / 4
Total

1. Write the word with a capital letter.

_____

_____ you go fast?
(**can**)

2. Add punctuation.

You are the best mom

3. Write the noun.

_____

I see a wet _____.
(**run** or **floor**)

4. Fill in the missing letter.

n ___ p

 #51172—180 Days of Language

NAME: _____

DIRECTIONS Read and answer each question.

1. Write the word with a capital letter.

_____

- - - - - - - - - -
_____ must go run.

(**you**)

1. Ⓨ Ⓝ

2. Add punctuation.

Where is the milk

2. Ⓨ Ⓝ

3. Ⓨ Ⓝ

3. Circle the verb.

The nest sits on the tree.

4. Ⓨ Ⓝ

___ / 4
Total

4. Fill in the missing letter.

h ___ p

NAME: _____

DIRECTIONS Read and answer each question.

1. Write the word with a capital letter.

_____

_____ you need a bank?
(do)

2. Add punctuation.

Do we need a tent

3. Circle the noun.

The desk is full.

4. Fill in the missing letter.

mo ____ n

  #51172—180 Days of Language

NAME: _____

DIRECTIONS Read and answer each question.

1. Circle the words that need capital letters.

do i need a cast?

2. Add punctuation.

That kid is fast

3. Circle the noun.

I see a car.

4. Fill in the missing letter.

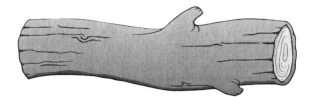

l ___ g

NAME: _____

DIRECTIONS Read and answer each question.

1. Write the word with a capital letter.

_____

_____ you use the sink?
(**can**)

2. Add punctuation.

The pump is slow

3. Circle the noun.

The cat rests.

4. Fill in the missing letter.

j _____ g

NAME: _____

DIRECTIONS Read and answer each question.

1. Circle the word that needs a capital letter.

Am i the last one?

2. Add punctuation.

Where will I send it

3. Circle the verb.

She moves the desk.

4. Fill in the missing letter.

h ___ t

SCORE

1. Ⓨ Ⓝ

2. Ⓨ Ⓝ

3. Ⓨ Ⓝ

4. Ⓨ Ⓝ

___ / 4
Total

NAME: _____

DIRECTIONS Read and answer each question.

1. Write the word with a capital letter.

_____

_____ you wink?

(**do**)

2. Add punctuation.

The list is long

3. Circle the verb.

The man helps me.

4. Fill in the missing letter.

h __ g

© Shell Education

NAME: _____

DIRECTIONS Read and answer each question.

1. Circle the word that needs a capital letter.

it will be fun.

2. Add punctuation.

Where are Mom and Dad

3. Circle the verb.

The crab walks.

4. Fill in the missing letter.

w ___ n

NAME: _____

DIRECTIONS Read and answer each question.

1. Circle the word that needs a capital letter.

i see the cat.

2. Add punctuation.

Can I rest

3. Write the noun.

The _____ went fast.

(**hop** or **car**)

4. Fill in the missing letter.

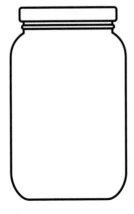

j ___ r

NAME: _____

DIRECTIONS Read and answer each question.

1. Write the word with a capital letter.

_____

– – – – – – can play in the sand.
(**we**)

2. Add punctuation.

The car went by

3. Write the plural noun.

_____

The – – – – – – – – – are red.
(**ant** or **ants**)

4. Fill in the missing letter.

___
m – – ___ m

NAME: _____

1. Ⓨ Ⓝ

2. Ⓨ Ⓝ

3. Ⓨ Ⓝ

4. Ⓨ Ⓝ

___ / 4
Total

DIRECTIONS Read and answer each question.

1. Circle the word that needs a capital letter.

Will i see my dad?

2. Add punctuation.

I must go now

3. Circle the nouns.

Sam sees a frog.

4. Fill in the missing letter.

s ___ n

NAME: _____

DIRECTIONS Read and answer each question.

1. Write the word with a capital letter.

_____

_____ is time for milk.
(**it**)

2. Add punctuation.

The dog is fast

3. Write the plural noun.

_____

The _____ are big.
(**bumps** or **bump**)

4. Fill in the missing letter.

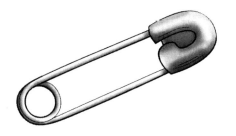

p ___ n

NAME: _____

SCORE

1. Ⓨ Ⓝ

2. Ⓨ Ⓝ

3. Ⓨ Ⓝ

4. Ⓨ Ⓝ

___ / 4
Total

DIRECTIONS Read and answer each question.

1. Circle the word that needs a capital letter.

Can i go with you?

2. Add punctuation.

I have cake to eat

3. Write the plural noun.

My _____ are best.
   (**vest** or **vests**)

4. Fill in the missing letter.

b ___ g

NAME: _____

DIRECTIONS Read and answer each question.

1. Write the word with a capital letter.

_____

_ _ _ eat food.
(i)

2. Add punctuation.

Where is the bank

3. Write the verb.

_____

Anna _____ a bike.
(**rides** or **shoe**)

4. Fill in the missing letter.

s _ _ nd

NAME: _____

SCORE

1. Ⓨ Ⓝ

2. Ⓨ Ⓝ

3. Ⓨ Ⓝ

4. Ⓨ Ⓝ

___ / 4
Total

1. Circle the word that needs a capital letter.

the flag is big.

2. Add punctuation.

The bee is mad

3. Write the noun.

_____

_ _ _ _ _ _ _ _ _ _ has a pen.

(**Max** or **Sees**)

4. Fill in the missing letter.

dr _ _ _ p

NAME: _____

DIRECTIONS Read and answer each question.

1. Write the word with a capital letter.

_____

_ _ _ _____ see colors.
(**i**)

2. Add punctuation.

I need to go last

3. Write the verb.

_____

Tim _____ the paper.
(**grabs** or **trees**)

4. Fill in the missing letter.

m _____ lk

NAME: _____

DIRECTIONS Read and answer each question.

1. Circle the word that needs a capital letter.

the boy is six.

2. Add punctuation.

Do you see my hand

3. Write the verb.

Ray _____ a car.

(**has** or **street**)

4. Fill in the missing letter.

_____ ask

 #51172—180 Days of Language

NAME: _____

DIRECTIONS Read and answer each question.

1. Circle the word that needs a capital letter.

i need a nap.

1. Ⓨ Ⓝ

2. Add punctuation.

Do not yell

2. Ⓨ Ⓝ

3. Ⓨ Ⓝ

3. Write the verb.

Bea _____ her doll.

(**pen** or **holds**)

4. Ⓨ Ⓝ

___ / 4
Total

4. Fill in the missing letter.

____ rum

NAME: _____

DIRECTIONS Read and answer each question.

1. Circle the word that needs a capital letter.

the book is short.

2. Add punctuation.

Do you like bugs

3. Circle the nouns.

My dad has a car.

4. Fill in the missing letter.

han ____ ____

© Shell Education

NAME: _____

DIRECTIONS Read and answer each question.

1. Write the word with a capital letter.

_____

_ _ _ _ _ _ _ _ _ _ me go home.
(let)

2. Add punctuation.

My dad is going home

3. Circle the verb.

Our dog plays.

4. Fill in the missing letter.

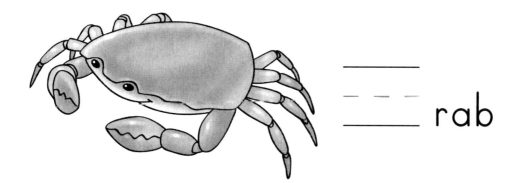

_ _ _ _ rab

NAME: _____

1. Ⓨ Ⓝ

2. Ⓨ Ⓝ

3. Ⓨ Ⓝ

4. Ⓨ Ⓝ

___ / 4
Total

DIRECTIONS Read and answer each question.

1. Write the word with a capital letter.

_____

_ _ _ _ _ _ _ _ _ _ can this be?
_____
(how)

2. Add punctuation.

I am so happy now

3. Circle the verb.

Books are fun.

4. Fill in the missing letter.

sl ____ d

NAME: _____

DIRECTIONS Read and answer each question.

1. Circle the word that needs a capital letter.

i saw a bird today.

2. Add punctuation.

The park was a lot of fun

3. Write the noun.

I like _____.
(apples or **walking)**

4. Fill in the missing letter.

sin ___

NAME: _____

1. Ⓨ Ⓝ

2. Ⓨ Ⓝ

3. Ⓨ Ⓝ

4. Ⓨ Ⓝ

___ / 4
Total

DIRECTIONS Read and answer each question.

1. Circle the word that needs a capital letter.

the play is very long.

2. Add punctuation.

Today is Monday

3. Circle the verb.

I ride a bike.

4. Fill in the missing letter.

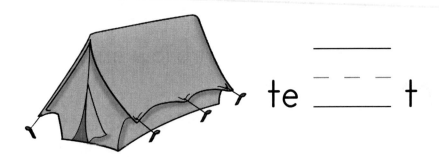

te ___ t

NAME: _____

DIRECTIONS Read and answer each question.

1. Write the word with a capital letter.

_____

__ __ __ __ __ __ you like to read?
(**do**)

1. Ⓨ Ⓝ

2. Add punctuation.

Can I go

2. Ⓨ Ⓝ

3. Ⓨ Ⓝ

3. Circle the verb.

I see a tree.

4. Ⓨ Ⓝ

___ / 4
Total

4. Fill in the missing letter.

fla __ __

NAME: _____

DIRECTIONS Read and answer each question.

1. Write the word with a capital letter.

_____

‾ ‾ ‾ ‾ ‾ ‾ ‾ ‾ ‾ ‾ bat is black.
_____
(**the**)

2. Add punctuation.

I need a new hat

3. Circle the noun.

I want a hat.

4. Fill in the missing letter.

‾ ‾ ‾
s ‾ ‾ ‾ im

#51172—180 Days of Language

NAME: _____

Read and answer each question.

1. Write the word with a capital letter.

_____

_ _ _ _ _ _ _ _ do we get home?
_____
(how)

1. Ⓨ Ⓝ

2. Ⓨ Ⓝ

3. Ⓨ Ⓝ

4. Ⓨ Ⓝ

___ / 4
Total

2. Add punctuation.

When is school over

3. Circle the verb.

I go to the park.

4. Fill in the missing letter.

ne _____ t

NAME: _____

SCORE

1. Ⓨ Ⓝ

2. Ⓨ Ⓝ

3. Ⓨ Ⓝ

4. Ⓨ Ⓝ

___ / 4
Total

DIRECTIONS Read and answer each question.

1. Write the word with a capital letter.

_____

- - - - - - - - - - -   I go with you?
_____
(**can**)

2. Add punctuation.

How are you doing

3. Circle the nouns.

We eat apples.

4. Fill in the missing letter.

lam ____

NAME: _____

DIRECTIONS Read and answer each question.

1. Write the word with a capital letter.

_____

_ _ _ _

_____ cat is on the mat.

(a)

2. Add punctuation.

I am very happy

3. Circle the verb.

I go to school.

4. Fill in the missing letter.

_____

_ _ _

p _____ g

NAME: _____

Read and answer each question.

SCORE

1. Ⓨ Ⓝ

2. Ⓨ Ⓝ

3. Ⓨ Ⓝ

4. Ⓨ Ⓝ

___ / 4
Total

1. Write the word with a capital letter.

_____

_ _ _ _
_____ will send it to you.
(i)

2. Add punctuation.

I like pizza a lot

3. Write the plural noun.

_____
The _ _ _ _ _ _ _ _ _ _ are slow.
(crab or **crabs)**

4. Fill in the missing letter.

_____
_ _ _
ram _____

NAME: _____

DIRECTIONS Read and answer each question.

1. Write the word with a capital letter.

_____

— — — — — — — list is very long.
(my)

2. Add punctuation.

Where is my hat

3. Write the plural noun.

_____

The — — — — — — — — — are big.
(bumps or **bump)**

4. Fill in the missing letter.

_____

— — —
_____ oy

NAME: _____

DIRECTIONS Read and answer each question.

1. Write the word with a capital letter.

_____

_ _ _ _
_____ need some help!
(i)

2. Add punctuation.

That really hurt

3. Write the plural noun.

_____

The _____ are full.
(**nest** or **nests**)

4. Fill in the missing letter.

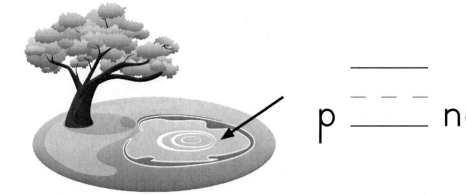

___
_ _ _
p _____ nd

NAME: _____

DIRECTIONS Read and answer each question.

1. Write the word with a capital letter.

_____

_ _ _ _ _ _ _ you want to swim?
(do)

2. Add punctuation.

My bike is red

3. Write the plural noun.

_____

Do you wear _ _ _ _ _ _ _ _ _ _?
(masks or mask)

4. Fill in the missing letter.

lis _ _ _

NAME: _____

DIRECTIONS   Read and answer each question.

1. Write the word with a capital letter.

_____

— — — — — — — — — —
_____ car must stop.
   (**the**)

2. Add punctuation.

The water is very cold

3. Write the plural noun.

_____
— — — — — — — — —
You have two _____.
                (**cat** or **cats**)

4. Fill in the missing letter.

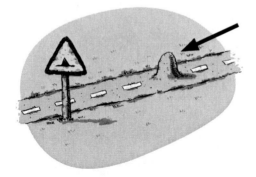

— — — —
b _____ mp

NAME: _____

DIRECTIONS Read and answer each question.

1. Circle the word that needs a capital letter.

May i have cake?

2. Add punctuation.

The tent is big

3. Write the plural noun.

You roll three _____.

(**balls** or **ball**)

4. Fill in the missing letter.

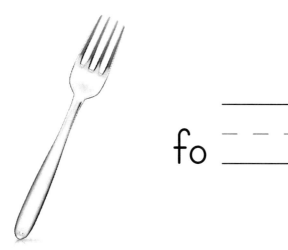

fo ___ k

NAME: _____

Read and answer each question.

SCORE

1. Ⓨ Ⓝ

2. Ⓨ Ⓝ

3. Ⓨ Ⓝ

4. Ⓨ Ⓝ

___ / 4
Total

1. Circle the word that needs a capital letter.

When will i go?

2. Add punctuation.

What is a hint

3. Write the plural noun.

You have two _____.

(**cakes** or **cake**)

4. Fill in the missing letter.

dra ____

NAME: _____

DIRECTIONS Read and answer each question.

1. Write the word with a capital letter.

_____

_____ play with others.
(**i**)

1. (Y) (N)

2. Add punctuation.

The van is very fast

2. (Y) (N)

3. Write the plural noun.

3. (Y) (N)

You have four _____.
(**game** or **games**)

4. (Y) (N)

___ / 4
Total

4. Fill in the missing letter.

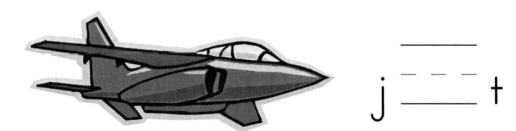

j ___ t

NAME: _____

SCORE

1. Ⓨ Ⓝ

2. Ⓨ Ⓝ

3. Ⓨ Ⓝ

4. Ⓨ Ⓝ

___ / 4
Total

DIRECTIONS Read and answer each question.

1. Write the word with a capital letter.

_____

_ _ _ _ _ read books.
(i)

2. Add punctuation.

Do you have a list

3. Write the plural noun.

_____

You have six _____.

(**rake** or **rakes**)

4. Fill in the missing letter.

st _____ r

#51172—180 Days of Language

NAME: _____

DIRECTIONS Read and answer each question.

1. Write the word with a capital letter.

_____

_ _ _ _ can climb.
(i)

2. Add punctuation.

The slug cannot move

3. Add the plural noun.

You have two _____.
(dime or **dimes)**

4. Fill in the missing letter.

b _ _ nd

NAME: _____

DIRECTIONS Read and answer each question.

SCORE

1. Ⓨ Ⓝ

2. Ⓨ Ⓝ

3. Ⓨ Ⓝ

4. Ⓨ Ⓝ

___ / 4
Total

1. Write the word with a capital letter.

_____

_____ is the time?
(what)

2. Add punctuation.

The tide is low

3. Circle the noun.

The bird goes by.

4. Fill in the missing letter.

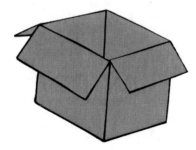

bo ___

NAME: _____

1. Write the word with a capital letter.

_____

_____ kite flies by.
(a)

2. Add punctuation.

How far is a mile

3. Write the verb.

_____

Pat _____ the book.
(**read** or **hair**)

4. Fill in the missing letter.

h ____ g

© Shell Education #51172—180 Days of Language

NAME: _____

SCORE

1. Ⓨ Ⓝ

2. Ⓨ Ⓝ

3. Ⓨ Ⓝ

4. Ⓨ Ⓝ

___ / 4
Total

DIRECTIONS Read and answer each question.

1. Write the word with a capital letter.

_____

‾ ‾ ‾ ‾ ‾ ‾ ‾
_____ car is mine.
(the)

2. Add punctuation.

Where is the hole

3. Write the verb.

_____

Sam ‾ ‾ ‾ ‾ ‾ ‾ ‾ ‾ to his home.
_____
(eye or **went)**

4. Fill in the missing letter.

___
‾ ‾ ‾
c ___ p

NAME: _____

| DIRECTIONS | Read and answer each question. |

1. Write the word with a capital letter.

_____

‾ ‾ ‾ ‾ ‾ ‾ mile is far.
(a)

2. Add punctuation.

That dog is very cute

3. Write the noun.

_____

The ‾ ‾ ‾ ‾ ‾ ‾ ‾ ‾ was fun.
(park or **speak)**

4. Fill in the missing letter.

v ‾ ‾ n

NAME: _____

DIRECTIONS   Read and answer each question.

1. Write the word with a capital letter.

_____

_____ mice are fun.
(the)

2. Add punctuation.

What is your hope

3. Write the verb.

_____

Anna _____ the pizza.
(hair or **eats)**

4. Fill in the missing letter.

a ____ t

NAME: _____

DIRECTIONS Read and answer each question.

1. Write the word with a capital letter.

_____

_ _ _ _ _ _ hope you can come.
(i)

2. Add punctuation.

Today is a good day

3. Write the plural noun.

You have two _____.

(rule or rules)

4. Fill in the missing letter.

fis _____

SCORE

1. Y N

2. Y N

3. Y N

4. Y N

___ / 4
Total

NAME: _____

DIRECTIONS Read and answer each question.

1. Write the word with a capital letter.

_____

_ _ _ _ _ _ _ _
_____ is my friend.
(kit)

2. Add punctuation.

The sale is over

3. Write the plural noun.

_____
_ _ _ _ _ _ _
There are two _____.
(bugs or **bug)**

4. Fill in the missing letter.

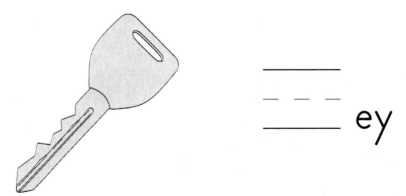

_ _ _ _
_ _ _ _
_____ ey

NAME: _____

DIRECTIONS Read and answer each question.

1. Write the word with a capital letter.

_____

_____ game is over.

(**the**)

2. Add punctuation.

Do you have a rope

3. Write the plural noun.

_____

There are two _____.

(**cages** or **cage**)

4. Fill in the missing letter.

r ___ ts

NAME: _____

DIRECTIONS Read and answer each question.

1. Write the word with a capital letter.

_____

_ _ _ lake can be cold.
(a)

2. Add punctuation.

When is June

3. Write the plural noun.

She has two _____.
(**capes** or **cape**)

4. Fill in the missing letter.

d ___ t

NAME: _____

DIRECTIONS Read and answer each question.

1. Write the word with a capital letter.

_____

------------------------ call me.

(**please**)

2. Add punctuation.

That is very rude

3. Write the plural noun.

_____

She needs two _____.

(**dime** or **dimes**)

4. Fill in the missing letter.

f ___ n

NAME: _____

DIRECTIONS Read and answer each question.

1. Write the word with a capital letter.

_____

_ _ _ _ _ _ _ _ _ _ _ _
_____ come home.
(**please**)

2. Add punctuation.

The flag is red

3. Circle the nouns.

The man had the ball.

4. Fill in the missing letter.

be __ t

NAME: _____

DIRECTIONS Read and answer each question.

1. Write the word with a capital letter.

_____

_ _ _ _ _ _ _ _ _ _ at that crab!
_____
(look)

1. Ⓨ Ⓝ

2. Add punctuation.

Can you play with a ball

2. Ⓨ Ⓝ

3. Ⓨ Ⓝ

3. Circle the nouns.

A bus is on the road.

4. Ⓨ Ⓝ

___ / 4
Total

4. Fill in the missing letter.

a _ _ _ m

NAME: _____

DIRECTIONS Read and answer each question.

1. Write the word with a capital letter.

_____

_ _ _ _ _ _ _ _ _ likes music.
(**she**)

2. Add punctuation.

The game was hard

3. Circle the nouns.

Where did the bird land on the nest?

4. Fill in the missing letter.

h ____ se

NAME: _____

DIRECTIONS Read and answer each question.

1. Write the word with a capital letter.

_____

_ _ _ _ _ _ _ _ _ _ _ _ _ is a bulb.
(here)

2. Add punctuation.

Today is a cold day

3. Circle the nouns.

A cat has a toy.

4. Fill in the missing letter.

ca ____ e

NAME: _____

DIRECTIONS   Read and answer each question.

1. Write the word with a capital letter.

_____

‾ ‾ ‾ ‾ ‾ ‾ ‾ ‾ ‾
_____ you ever done that?
(**have**)

2. Add punctuation.

I like apples

3. Circle the nouns.

The van had four tires.

4. Fill in the missing letter.

ca ‾ ‾ ‾ ‾ e

NAME: _____

DIRECTIONS Read and answer each question.

1. Write the word with a capital letter.

_____

_ _ _ _ _ _ _

_____ at my hand.

(look)

2. Add punctuation.

The dog loves to walk

3. Circle the verb.

Val sees a rose.

4. Fill in the missing letter.

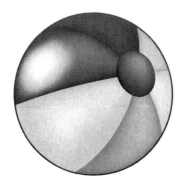

ba _ _ _ l

NAME: _____

SCORE

1. Ⓨ Ⓝ

2. Ⓨ Ⓝ

3. Ⓨ Ⓝ

4. Ⓨ Ⓝ

___ / 4
Total

DIRECTIONS Read and answer each question.

1. Write the word with a capital letter.

_____

_ _ _ _ _ _ dad is tall.
_____
(**my**)

2. Add punctuation.

That is way too loud

3. Circle the verb.

Eve likes movies.

4. Fill in the missing letter.

ro __ __ e

NAME: _____

DIRECTIONS Read and answer each question.

1. Write the word with a capital letter.

_____

‾ ‾ ‾ ‾ ‾ ‾ ‾ to school today.
(**go**)

2. Add punctuation.

Who likes to play ball

3. Circle the verb.

Ned needs his book.

4. Fill in the missing letter.

‾ ‾ ‾
co ____ e

SCORE

1. Ⓨ Ⓝ

2. Ⓨ Ⓝ

3. Ⓨ Ⓝ

4. Ⓨ Ⓝ

___ / 4
Total

NAME: _____

DIRECTIONS Read and answer each question.

1. Write the word with a capital letter.

_____

_____ you have the time?
(**do**)

2. Add punctuation.

I do not know his name

3. Circle the verb.

Min said yes.

4. Fill in the missing letter.

le ___ f

#51172—180 Days of Language

NAME: _____

DIRECTIONS Read and answer each question.

1. Write the word with a capital letter.

_____

_____ are you sad?

(**why**)

2. Add punctuation.

The apple is red

3. Circle the verb.

The dog barks.

4. Fill in the missing letter.

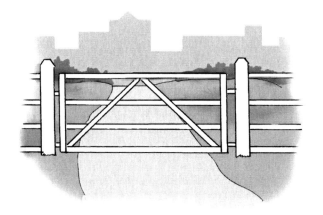 ga ___ e

NAME: _____

SCORE

1. Ⓨ Ⓝ

2. Ⓨ Ⓝ

3. Ⓨ Ⓝ

4. Ⓨ Ⓝ

___ / 4
Total

DIRECTIONS Read and answer each question.

1. Write your first name.

_____

_____

_____

2. Add punctuation.

I like to swim

3. Write the pronoun.

_____

_____ cut the paper.

(He or **Run)**

4. Fill in the missing letter.

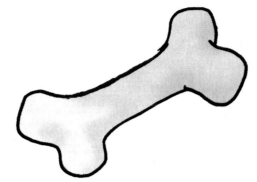

bo ____ e

#51172—180 Days of Language   © *Shell Education*

NAME: _____

DIRECTIONS Read and answer each question.

1. Write the word with a capital letter.

_____

_ _ _ _ _ am 5 years old.
(**i**)

2. Add punctuation.

Can I go

3. Write the verb.

_____

Rob _____ his food.
(**ate** or **her**)

4. Fill in the missing letter.

ca _____

NAME: _____

SCORE

1. Ⓨ Ⓝ

2. Ⓨ Ⓝ

3. Ⓨ Ⓝ

4. Ⓨ Ⓝ

___ / 4
Total

DIRECTIONS Read and answer each question.

1. Write your teacher's name.

_____

_ _ _ _ _ _ _ _ _ _ _ _ _ _ _ _

_____

2. Add punctuation.

That was a great game

3. Write the noun.

The _____ is very fast.
     (**cat** or **hot**)

4. Fill in the missing letter.

bi ___ d

NAME: _____

DIRECTIONS Read and answer each question.

1. Write the name of a month.

_____

— — — — — — — — — — — — —

_____

1. Ⓨ Ⓝ

2. Ⓨ Ⓝ

2. Add punctuation.

When is lunch

3. Ⓨ Ⓝ

4. Ⓨ Ⓝ

___ / 4
Total

3. Write the noun.

The _____ is pink.

(speeding or **car)**

4. Fill in the missing letter.

ra ___ e

NAME: _____

DIRECTIONS Read and answer each question.

SCORE

1. Ⓨ Ⓝ

2. Ⓨ Ⓝ

3. Ⓨ Ⓝ

4. Ⓨ Ⓝ

___ / 4
Total

1. Write the word with a capital letter.

_____

_ _ _ _ _ _ _ _ _ _ are you?
(**how**)

2. Add punctuation.

I want to hop

3. Write the verb.

_____

The cat _____ away.
(**pen** or **ran**)

4. Fill in the missing letter.

hi _ _ _ e

NAME: _____

DIRECTIONS Read and answer each question.

1. Circle the words that need capital letters.

"look at me," i said.

2. Add punctuation.

Where is the spot

3. Circle the verb.

The vet works hard.

4. Fill in the missing letters.

b _ _ e

NAME: _____

Read and answer each question.

SCORE

1. Ⓨ Ⓝ

2. Ⓨ Ⓝ

3. Ⓨ Ⓝ

4. Ⓨ Ⓝ

___ / 4
Total

1. Circle the words that need capital letters.

"this is fun," i said.

2. Add punctuation.

Where will you go

3. Circle the verb.

My mom walks fast.

4. Fill in the missing letter.

c ___ t

 #51172—180 Days of Language

NAME: _____

SCORE

1. Ⓨ Ⓝ

2. Ⓨ Ⓝ

3. Ⓨ Ⓝ

4. Ⓨ Ⓝ

___ / 4
Total

DIRECTIONS Read and answer each question.

1. Circle the words that need capital letters.

when do i get to go?

2. Add punctuation.

I am very happy to see you

3. Circle the nouns.

Miss Kane is my teacher.

4. Fill in the missing letter.

fro _____

NAME: _____

DIRECTIONS Read and answer each question.

1. Ⓨ Ⓝ

2. Ⓨ Ⓝ

3. Ⓨ Ⓝ

4. Ⓨ Ⓝ

___ / 4
Total

1. Circle the words that need capital letters.

i said that i will help.

2. Add punctuation.

I ate rice and beans

3. Circle the verb.

The jay sits in the nest.

4. Fill in the missing letter.

s ____ ug

  #51172—180 Days of Language

NAME: _____

DIRECTIONS Read and answer each question.

1. Circle the word that needs a capital letter.

Can i get over the bump?

1. Ⓨ Ⓝ

2. Add punctuation.

Watch out for the car

2. Ⓨ Ⓝ

3. Circle the nouns.

Hal has a book.

3. Ⓨ Ⓝ

4. Ⓨ Ⓝ

___ / 4
Total

4. Fill in the missing letter.

doo ____

NAME: _____

DIRECTIONS Read and answer each question.

1. Write the word with a capital letter.

_____

_ _ _ _ _ _ _ _ _ _ _ _ _ is the first page.
(**this**)

2. Add punctuation.

Where is my mom

3. Circle the nouns.

Jan likes the movie.

4. Fill in the missing letter.

b _ _ _ th

  #51172—180 Days of Language

NAME: _____

Read and answer each question.

1. Write the word with a capital letter.

_____

‾ ‾ ‾
_____ cap is on my head.
(a)

1. Ⓨ Ⓝ

2. Ⓨ Ⓝ

2. Add punctuation.

The crab moves

3. Ⓨ Ⓝ

4. Ⓨ Ⓝ

3. Circle the verb.

Kim goes to her room.

___ / 4
Total

4. Fill in the missing letter.

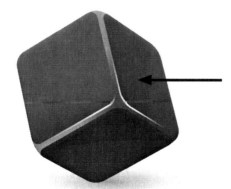

‾ ‾ ‾
s _____ de

NAME: _____

DIRECTIONS Read and answer each question.

1. Write the word with a capital letter.

_____

‾ ‾ ‾ ‾ ‾ ‾ ‾ ‾ ‾ I see you?
_____
     (will)

2. Add punctuation.

The pig has to eat

3. Circle the nouns.

Fred has a bag.

4. Fill in the missing letter.

f ‾‾‾ sh

NAME: _____

DIRECTIONS Read and answer each question.

1. Write the word with a capital letter.

_____

‾ ‾ ‾ ‾ ‾ ‾ ‾
_____ can do it.
(**she**)

2. Add punctuation.

That is too fast

3. Circle the nouns.

Evan likes to play soccer.

4. Fill in the missing letter.

‾ ‾ ‾
l _ _ _ on

SCORE

1. Ⓨ Ⓝ

2. Ⓨ Ⓝ

3. Ⓨ Ⓝ

4. Ⓨ Ⓝ

___ / 4
Total

NAME: _____

DIRECTIONS Read and answer each question.

1. Write the word with a capital letter.

_____

‾ ‾ ‾ ‾ ‾ ‾ ‾ ‾ ‾ ‾ ‾ ‾

_____ may be mad.

(**he**)

2. Add punctuation.

Who can help me

3. Circle the nouns.

Nan has a baby.

4. Fill in the missing letter.

d _ _ _ sh

NAME: _____

DIRECTIONS Read and answer each question.

1. Write the word with a capital letter.

_____

- - - - - - - - - - - - - ice is cold.
_____
(**the**)

2. Add punctuation.

When will school start

3. Circle the nouns.

Ava went to bed.

4. Fill in the missing letter.

s ____ ng

NAME: _____

DIRECTIONS Read and answer each question.

1. Write the word with a capital letter.

_____

_ _ _ _ _ _ the dog in his cage.
_____
(**put**)

2. Add punctuation.

The bunny went away

3. Circle the nouns.

Pam needs a lunch.

4. Fill in the missing letter.

_____
_ _ _
c _____ w

 #51172—180 Days of Language

NAME: _____

DIRECTIONS Read and answer each question.

1. Write the word with a capital letter.

_____

_ _ _ _ _____ love you very much!
(i)

2. Add punctuation.

Why do you need the hat

3. Circle the noun.

The coin is shiny.

4. Fill in the missing letter.

wor _ _ _ _

NAME: _____

Read and answer each question.

SCORE

1. Ⓨ Ⓝ

2. Ⓨ Ⓝ

3. Ⓨ Ⓝ

4. Ⓨ Ⓝ

___ / 4
Total

1. Write the word with a capital letter.

_____

— — — — — — — — _____ you play with me?
(will)

2. Add punctuation.

The band is loud

3. Circle the noun.

Jane was so kind.

4. Fill in the missing letter.

e ___ e

NAME: _____

DIRECTIONS Read and answer each question.

1. Write the word with a capital letter.

_____

_____ corn was good!
(**the**)

2. Add punctuation.

The plant is tall

3. Circle the nouns.

The train went by the road.

4. Fill in the missing letter.

f _____ ce

SCORE

1. Ⓨ Ⓝ

2. Ⓨ Ⓝ

3. Ⓨ Ⓝ

4. Ⓨ Ⓝ

___ / 4
Total

NAME: _____

Read and answer each question.

SCORE

1. Ⓨ Ⓝ

2. Ⓨ Ⓝ

3. Ⓨ Ⓝ

4. Ⓨ Ⓝ

___ / 4
Total

1. Write the word with a capital letter.

_____

_ _ _ _ _ _ deer came over to me.
(a)

2. Add punctuation.

Kate was very mad

3. Circle the noun.

The car sped by.

4. Fill in the missing letter.

_ _ _ _ _
je ___ p

 #51172—180 Days of Language

NAME: _____

DIRECTIONS Read and answer each question.

1. Write the word with a capital letter.

_____

_ _ _ _ _ _
_____ mice were gray.
(**the**)

2. Add punctuation.

Why was the tire flat

3. Circle the noun.

The dog plays.

4. Fill in the missing letter.

w _____ ve
_ _ _ _

SCORE

1. Ⓨ Ⓝ

2. Ⓨ Ⓝ

3. Ⓨ Ⓝ

4. Ⓨ Ⓝ

___ / 4
Total

NAME: _____

1. Ⓨⓝ

2. Ⓨⓝ

3. Ⓨⓝ

4. Ⓨⓝ

___ / 4
Total

DIRECTIONS Read and answer each question.

1. Write the word with a capital letter.

_____

_ _ _ _ _ _
_____ you help me?

(can)

2. Add punctuation.

Is that a rose

3. Circle the noun.

The creek is cold.

4. Fill in the missing letter.

_____
_ _ _
sea _____

NAME: _____

DIRECTIONS Read and answer each question.

1. Write the word with a capital letter.

_____

‾ ‾ ‾ ‾ ‾ ‾
_____ you hold it?
(will)

2. Add punctuation.

I hope it is true

3. Circle the verb.

My feet tap.

4. Fill in the missing letter.

bi _____ e

SCORE

1. Ⓨ Ⓝ

2. Ⓨ Ⓝ

3. Ⓨ Ⓝ

4. Ⓨ Ⓝ

___ / 4
Total

NAME: _____

DIRECTIONS Read and answer each question.

1. Write the word with a capital letter.

_____

_ _ _ _ _ _ _ dog is slow.
(my)

2. Add punctuation.

Does the cat bite

3. Circle the verb.

The ice cream drips.

4. Fill in the missing letter.

ro ____ e

NAME: _____

DIRECTIONS Read and answer each question.

1. Circle the word that needs a capital letter.

Do i need to say it?

2. Add punctuation.

Jay sees a bug

3. Circle the verb.

Lee plans his work.

4. Fill in the missing letter.

mea ____

SCORE

1. Ⓨ Ⓝ

2. Ⓨ Ⓝ

3. Ⓨ Ⓝ

4. Ⓨ Ⓝ

___ / 4
Total

NAME: _____

Read and answer each question.

SCORE

1. Ⓨ Ⓝ

2. Ⓨ Ⓝ

3. Ⓨ Ⓝ

4. Ⓨ Ⓝ

___ / 4
Total

1. Circle the words that need capital letters.

how will i know?

2. Add punctuation.

Sam needs a hug

3. Circle the verb.

Jake runs away.

4. Fill in the missing letter.

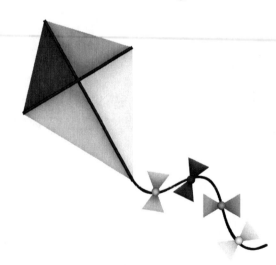

ki ____ e

NAME: _____

DIRECTIONS Read and answer each question.

1. Circle the word that needs a capital letter.

May i have that?

2. Add punctuation.

Who is in the car

3. Circle the verb.

The ice cube melts.

4. Fill in the missing letter.

f __ __ ld

NAME: _____

Read and answer each question.

SCORE

1. Y N

2. Y N

3. Y N

4. Y N

___ / 4
Total

1. Circle the word that needs a capital letter.

i think she is nice.

2. Add punctuation.

Watch out

3. Circle the verb.

Dave walks to his car.

4. Fill in the missing letter.

m ____ w

NAME: _____

DIRECTIONS Read and answer each question.

1. Circle the word that needs a capital letter.

i see the new rug.

2. Add punctuation.

I miss you

3. Circle the verb.

Nate sees a bird.

4. Fill in the missing letter.

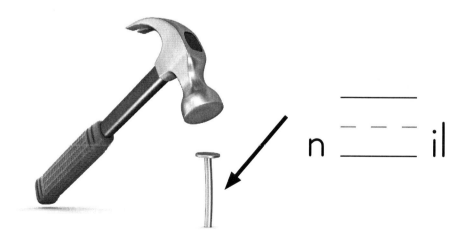

n ___ il

SCORE

1. Ⓨ Ⓝ

2. Ⓨ Ⓝ

3. Ⓨ Ⓝ

4. Ⓨ Ⓝ

___ / 4
Total

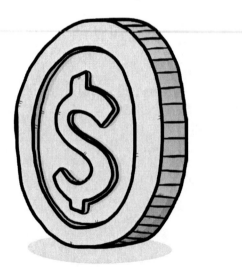

NAME: _____

DIRECTIONS Read and answer each question.

SCORE

1. Ⓨ Ⓝ

2. Ⓨ Ⓝ

3. Ⓨ Ⓝ

4. Ⓨ Ⓝ

___ / 4
Total

1. Circle the word that needs a capital letter.

i need help.

2. Add punctuation.

Do you want a red one

3. Circle the verb.

Jim feels happy.

4. Fill in the missing letter.

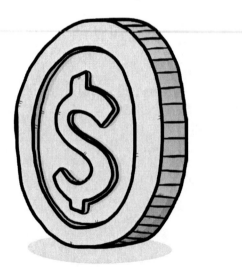 _____ oin

#51172—180 Days of Language   © Shell Education

NAME: _____

DIRECTIONS Read and answer each question.

1. Circle the word that needs a capital letter.

we can bake a pie.

2. Add punctuation.

Do you need a tack

3. Circle the verb.

The cat can jump.

4. Fill in the missing letter.

b ___ d

NAME: _____

DIRECTIONS Read and answer each question.

1. Circle the word that needs a capital letter.

1. Ⓨ Ⓝ

my mom is not home.

2. Ⓨ Ⓝ

2. Add punctuation.

I am very mad

3. Ⓨ Ⓝ

3. Circle the verb.

4. Ⓨ Ⓝ

The girl reads the book.

____ / 4
Total

4. Fill in the missing letter.

wi ___ k

#51172—180 Days of Language   © Shell Education

NAME: _____

DIRECTIONS Read and answer each question.

1. Circle the word that needs a capital letter.

max is kind to me.

2. Add punctuation.

Why are you sad

3. Circle the nouns.

Rick walks to school.

4. Fill in the missing letter.

_ _ _ ee

NAME: _____

DIRECTIONS Read and answer each question.

1. Circle the word that needs a capital letter.

i hope to see the doll.

2. Add punctuation.

Do not go home

3. Circle the verb.

My mom gave me a gift.

4. Fill in the missing letter.

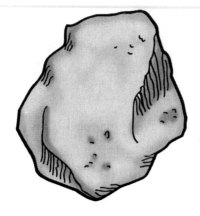

r ___ ck

NAME: _____

DIRECTIONS Read and answer each question.

1. Circle the word that needs a capital letter.

sam is my friend.

2. Add punctuation.

How will I get that done

3. Circle the nouns.

The home is on a street.

4. Fill in the missing letter.

d ___ ck

NAME: _____

DIRECTIONS Read and answer each question.

1. Circle the word that needs a capital letter.

Do i need to be here?

2. Add punctuation.

That is very scary

3. Circle the verb.

I wrote a code.

4. Fill in the missing letter.

cl ___ ck

NAME: _____

DIRECTIONS Read and answer each question.

SCORE

1. Circle the words that need capital letters.

can i have that?

1. Ⓨ Ⓝ

2. Ⓨ Ⓝ

2. Add punctuation.

The cat is lazy

3. Ⓨ Ⓝ

4. Ⓨ Ⓝ

3. Circle the noun.

The plant grows tall.

___ / 4
Total

4. Fill in the missing letter.

r ___ ng

NAME: _____

DIRECTIONS Read and answer each question.

SCORE

1. Ⓨ Ⓝ

2. Ⓨ Ⓝ

3. Ⓨ Ⓝ

4. Ⓨ Ⓝ

___/ 4
Total

1. Circle the word that needs a capital letter.

my pal is at home.

2. Add punctuation.

The robe is on a hook

3. Circle the verb.

I rode in the car.

4. Fill in the missing letter.

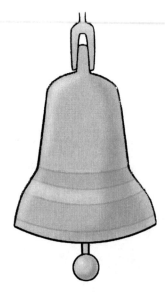

b ___ ll

   #51172—180 Days of Language

NAME: _____

DIRECTIONS Read and answer each question.

1. Circle the word that needs a capital letter.

jill wants to go to school.

2. Add punctuation.

Where is my note

3. Circle the verb.

She will dine now.

4. Fill in the missing letter.

p _____ ck

SCORE

1. Ⓨ Ⓝ

2. Ⓨ Ⓝ

3. Ⓨ Ⓝ

4. Ⓨ Ⓝ

___ / 4
Total

NAME: _____

DIRECTIONS Read and answer each question.

1. Write the word with a capital letter.

_____

_ _ _ _ _ _ _ _ mop is in the pail.
(my)

2. Add punctuation.

Who will come over and play

3. Circle the noun.

The baby is sad.

4. Fill in the missing letter.

f _ _ _ x

NAME: _____

DIRECTIONS Read and answer each question.

1. Write the word with a capital letter.

_____

– – – – – – – – – –
_____ tent is full of dust.
(**the**)

2. Add punctuation.

I am very happy with you

3. Circle the verb.

Jan hides from me.

4. Fill in the missing letter.

___
– – –
sn ____ il

NAME: _____

DIRECTIONS Read and answer each question.

1. Write the word with a capital letter.

_____

- - - - -
_____ you send it to me?
(will)

2. Add punctuation.

I will use the hose

3. Circle the verb.

Dan hikes up the hill.

4. Fill in the missing letter.

_ _ _
_____ eal

NAME: _____

DIRECTIONS Read and answer each question.

1. Write the word with a capital letter.

_____

‾ ‾ ‾ ‾ ‾ ‾ ‾ ‾ ‾ ‾
_____ can we swim?
　　(**when**)

2. Add punctuation.

Do we go in June

3. Circle the verb.

Hank rides to work.

4. Fill in the missing letter.

tu ___ e

NAME: _____

DIRECTIONS Read and answer each question.

1. Write the word with a capital letter.

_____

_ _ _ _ _ _
_____ you need help?
(do)

2. Add punctuation.

What is that tune

3. Circle the verb.

June piles the paper.

4. Fill in the missing letter.

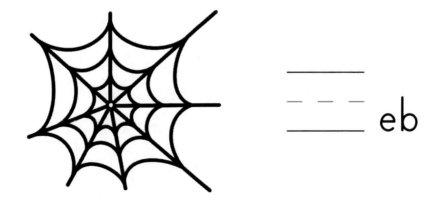

_____
_ _ _ eb
_____

NAME: _____

DIRECTIONS Read and answer each question.

1. Write the word with a capital letter.

_____

_ _ _ _ _ _ _ _ _ _ _ _ do I make that?
(how)

2. Add punctuation.

Do not let go of the rope

3. Write the plural noun.

He has three _____.
(bone or **bones)**

4. Fill in the missing letter.

_____
_ _ _ op

NAME: _____

DIRECTIONS Read and answer each question.

1. Write the word with a capital letter.

_____

_____ want to pick a rose.
(i)

2. Add punctuation.

Fly the kite for me

3. Write the plural noun.

_____

I see six _____.
(tiles or **tile)**

4. Fill in the missing letter.

r _____ nk

NAME: _____

DIRECTIONS Read and answer each question.

1. Write the word with a capital letter.

_____

_ _ _ _ _ _ _ _ _ _ the book to bed.
(**take**)

2. Add punctuation.

I want to bake a cake

3. Write the plural noun.

_ _ _ _ _ _ _ _ _ _ _ _

I have five pine _____.
(**cone** or **cones**)

4. Fill in the missing letter.

t _ _ _ b

NAME: _____

DIRECTIONS   Read and answer each question.

1. Ⓨ Ⓝ

2. Ⓨ Ⓝ

3. Ⓨ Ⓝ

4. Ⓨ Ⓝ

___ / 4
Total

1. Write the word with a capital letter.

_____

$\overline{}$ not poke me!
(do)

2. Add punctuation.

The race is over

3. Write the plural noun.

Let's play ten $\overline{}$.
(games or **game)**

4. Fill in the missing letter.

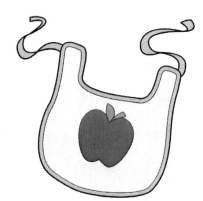

b ___ b

 #51172—*180 Days of Language*

NAME: _____

DIRECTIONS Read and answer each question.

1. Write the word with a capital letter.

_____

___ ___ ___ woke up at six.
(i)

2. Add punctuation.

Jake got in the car

3. Write the plural noun.

I can see four _____.
(**race** or **races**)

4. Fill in the missing letter.

wago ___

NAME: _____

DIRECTIONS Read and answer each question.

1. Write the word with a capital letter.

_____

_ _ _
_____ can hear the tune.
(i)

2. Add punctuation.

Is it Monday

3. Write the plural noun.

_____

I see five _____.
(lakes or **lake)**

4. Fill in the missing letter.

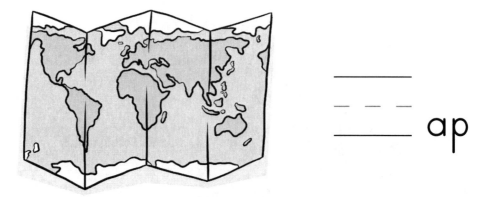

_____
_ _ _
_____ ap

NAME: _____

Read and answer each question.

1. Write the word with a capital letter.

_____

_ _ _ _ _ _ bell will ring.
    (**the**)

2. Add punctuation.

I pet the dog

3. Write the plural noun.

_____

There are ten _____.
    (**waves** or **wave**)

4. Fill in the missing letter.

_ _ _ ice

SCORE

1. Ⓨ Ⓝ

2. Ⓨ Ⓝ

3. Ⓨ Ⓝ

4. Ⓨ Ⓝ

___ / 4
Total

NAME: _____

DIRECTIONS Read and answer each question.

1. Write the word with a capital letter.

_____

_____ sure looks good.
   (that)

2. Add punctuation.

I am very happy

3. Write the plural noun.

_____

I have six _____.
                (dime or **dimes)**

4. Fill in the missing letter.

l __ __ me

NAME: _____

DIRECTIONS Read and answer each question.

1. Write the word with a capital letter.

_____

_____ Hal play?
(**can**)

2. Add punctuation.

I want pizza

3. Write the plural noun.

I took six _____.
(**bites** or **bite**)

4. Fill in the missing letter.

___ ___ ail

SCORE

1. Ⓨ Ⓝ

2. Ⓨ Ⓝ

3. Ⓨ Ⓝ

4. Ⓨ Ⓝ

___ / 4
Total

NAME: _____

SCORE

1. Ⓨ Ⓝ

2. Ⓨ Ⓝ

3. Ⓨ Ⓝ

4. Ⓨ Ⓝ

___ / 4
Total

DIRECTIONS Read and answer each question.

1. Write the word with a capital letter.

_____

_ _ _ _
_____ the dog black or brown?
(**is**)

2. Add punctuation.

Is it raining

3. Write the plural noun.

_____

The _____ are tall.
(**poles** or **pole**)

4. Fill in the missing letter.

_____
_ _ _
n ____ se

NAME: _____

DIRECTIONS Read and answer each question.

1. Write the word with a capital letter.

_____

_ _ _ _ _
_____ you want some cake?
(**do**)

2. Add punctuation.

The hive was buzzing

3. Circle the verb.

The kitten sat in the yard.

4. Which word is spelled correctly?

cat

catt

NAME: _____

DIRECTIONS Read and answer each question.

1. Write the word with a capital letter.

_____

_ _ _ _ _ _ _ _ _ _ _ _ _ is a good friend.
(jack)

2. Add punctuation.

Does this work

3. Write the verb.

_____

The girl _ _ _ _ _ _ _ _ _ _ _ the doll.
(hugs or **hug)**

4. Which word is spelled correctly?

het

hit

NAME: _____

DIRECTIONS Read and answer each question.

1. Write the word with a capital letter.

_____

_ _ _ _ _ _ _ _ _ _ _
_____ was a hot day!
(that)

2. Add punctuation.

The beach was too cold

3. Circle the noun.

The team works hard.

4. Which word is spelled correctly?

tope

top

NAME: _____

1. Ⓨ Ⓝ

2. Ⓨ Ⓝ

3. Ⓨ Ⓝ

4. Ⓨ Ⓝ

___ / 4
Total

DIRECTIONS Read and answer each question.

1. Write the word with a capital letter.

_____

‗ ‗ ‗ ‗ ‗ ‗ ‗ ‗ does not like to lose.
_____
(ned)

2. Add punctuation.

How can we get home

3. Write the verb.

_____

The hare ‗ ‗ ‗ ‗ ‗ ‗ ‗ fast.
_____
(red or **runs)**

4. Which word is spelled correctly?

mom

momm

NAME: _____

DIRECTIONS Read and answer each question.

1. Write the word with a capital letter.

_____

‾ ‾ ‾ ‾ ‾ ‾ ‾ ‾
_____ does not like bikes.
(**fran**)

2. Add punctuation.

This is the best day ever

3. Write the pronoun.

_____

‾ ‾ ‾ ‾ ‾ ‾ ‾ ‾
_____ took care of me.
(**She** or **Karen**)

4. Which word is spelled correctly?

rat

ratt

SCORE

1. Ⓨ Ⓝ

2. Ⓨ Ⓝ

3. Ⓨ Ⓝ

4. Ⓨ Ⓝ

___ / 4
Total

NAME: _____

DIRECTIONS   Read and answer each question.

1. Write the word with a capital letter.

_____

‾ ‾ ‾ ‾ ‾ ‾ ‾ ‾ ‾ ‾ ‾
_____ bird is in the sky.
(the)

2. Add punctuation.

Who is your teacher

3. Circle the nouns.

The man likes the book.

4. Which word is spelled correctly?

rak

rake

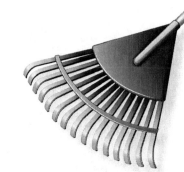

NAME: _____

DIRECTIONS Read and answer each question.

1. Write the word with a capital letter.

_____

‾ ‾ ‾ ‾ ‾ ‾ ‾ ‾
_____ apple is good to eat.
(an)

2. Add punctuation.

Look at that car zoom by

3. Circle the verb.

Ken asked his friend over.

4. Which word is spelled correctly?

clip

clp

NAME: _____

DIRECTIONS Read and answer each question.

1. Write the word with a capital letter.

_____

_ _ _ _ _ _
_____ day, I will go there.
(**one**)

2. Add punctuation.

Where is your house

3. Write the noun.

_____

The _ _ _ _ _ _ works hard.
_____
(**boy** or **blue**)

4. Which word is spelled correctly?

drp

drip

NAME: _____

Read and answer each question.

1. Write the word with a capital letter.

_____

_____ kids are nice.

(**some**)

2. Add punctuation.

The story was too short

3. Write the noun.

_____

A _____ is fun to play with.

(**ran** or **toy**)

4. Which word is spelled correctly?

shop

shp

NAME: _____

DIRECTIONS Read and answer each question.

1. Write the word with a capital letter.

_____

_____ time, I will go first.
(**next**)

2. Add punctuation.

I want to go home right now

3. Circle the nouns.

The boat came to shore.

4. Which word is spelled correctly?

frg

frog

DIRECTIONS Read and answer each question.

1. Write the word with a capital letter.

_____

_____ dinner, I sleep.
    (after)

2. Add punctuation.

Are you going home

3. Write the verb.

_____

Rick loves to _____.
            (hair or **play)**

4. Which word is spelled correctly?

snap

snp

NAME: _____

SCORE

1. Ⓨ Ⓝ

2. Ⓨ Ⓝ

3. Ⓨ Ⓝ

4. Ⓨ Ⓝ

___/ 4
Total

1. Write the word with a capital letter.

_____

_ _ _ _ _ _ _ _ _ _ _ _ _ _ _ _ _ _
_____ you for my gift.
(**thank**)

2. Add punctuation.

May feels very sad

3. Write the noun.

_ _ _ _ _ _ _ _ _ _ _ _
My dad washed my _____.
(**green** or **dog**)

4. Which word is spelled correctly?

drm

drum

NAME: _____

DIRECTIONS Read and answer each question.

1. Write the word with a capital letter.

_____

_ _ _ _ _ _ _ _ _ I help you?
(**may**)

2. Add punctuation.

When is the party

3. Write the noun.

_____

The _ _ _ _ _ _ _ helps the class.
(**man** or **skip**)

4. Which word is spelled correctly?

bike

bice

NAME: _____

DIRECTIONS Read and answer each question.

1. Write the word with a capital letter.

_____

_____ the book down.
(**put**)

2. Add punctuation.

She will clean her room

3. Write the verb.

_____

My mom _____ hugs.
(**food** or **gives**)

4. Which word is spelled correctly?

brd

bird

NAME: _____

DIRECTIONS Read and answer each question.

1. Write the word with a capital letter.

_____

_____ being so loud!
(stop)

2. Add punctuation.

Can I play with your toys

3. Write the noun.

_____

Maria hugs her _____.
(red or **cat)**

4. Which word is spelled correctly?

plae

play

NAME: _____

DIRECTIONS Read and answer each question.

1. Circle the words that need capital letters.

when can i go home?

2. Add punctuation.

I like to drink milk

3. Write the plural noun.

She needs three _____.

(**limes** or **lime**)

4. Which word is spelled correctly?

slow

slo

NAME: _____

DIRECTIONS Read and answer each question.

1. Circle the words that need capital letters.

do i need to run today?

2. Add punctuation.

I need to take a rest

3. Write the plural noun.

I love my _____.

(**pets** or **pet**)

4. Which word is spelled correctly?

hop

hopp

NAME: _____

DIRECTIONS Read and answer each question.

1. Circle the words that need capital letters.

will i ever find out the secret?

2. Add punctuation.

May I have more time

3. Write the plural noun.

Evan read four _____.

(**book** or **books**)

4. Which word is spelled correctly?

stopp

stop

#51172—180 Days of Language   © Shell Education

NAME: _____

DIRECTIONS Read and answer each question.

1. Circle the word that needs a capital letter.

May i go to the store with you?

1. Ⓨ Ⓝ

2. Add punctuation.

What is your name

2. Ⓨ Ⓝ

3. Ⓨ Ⓝ

3. Write the plural noun.

I want two _____.

(**bike** or **bikes**)

4. Ⓨ Ⓝ

___ / 4
Total

4. Which word is spelled correctly?

bell

bel

NAME: _____

DIRECTIONS Read and answer each question.

1. Circle the words that need capital letters.

who can i help today?

2. Add punctuation.

I ate my lunch

3. Write the plural noun.

There are three _____.

(**desks** or **desk**)

4. Which word is spelled correctly?

booke

book

NAME: _____

DIRECTIONS Read and answer each question.

SCORE

1. Circle the words that need capital letters.

when do i go to sleep?

1. Ⓨ Ⓝ

2. Add punctuation.

2. Ⓨ Ⓝ

Who will be on my team

3. Ⓨ Ⓝ

3. Write the verb.

4. Ⓨ Ⓝ

I _____ to school.

(**skip** or **home**)

___ / 4
Total

4. Which word is spelled correctly?

boy

boi

NAME: _____

Read and answer each question.

SCORE

1. Ⓨ Ⓝ

2. Ⓨ Ⓝ

3. Ⓨ Ⓝ

4. Ⓨ Ⓝ

___/ 4
Total

1. Circle the words that need capital letters.

how can i do that?

2. Add punctuation.

I really love to go to the beach

3. Write the verb.

Birds _____ in the sky.

(**leg** or **fly**)

4. Which word is spelled correctly?

cap

caip

 #51172—180 Days of Language

NAME: _____

DIRECTIONS Read and answer each question.

1. Circle the words that need capital letters.

do i need to get shots today?

1. Ⓨ Ⓝ

2. Add punctuation.

Can we have pizza every day

2. Ⓨ Ⓝ

3. Ⓨ Ⓝ

3. Write the pronoun.

_____

‾ ‾ ‾ ‾ ‾ ‾ ‾ ‾ ‾ ‾ ‾ ‾ ‾ ‾
_____ is on a bike.
(**Tom** or **He**)

4. Ⓨ Ⓝ

___ / 4
Total

4. Which word is spelled correctly?

foode

food

NAME: _____

1. Ⓨ Ⓝ

2. Ⓨ Ⓝ

3. Ⓨ Ⓝ

4. Ⓨ Ⓝ

___ / 4
Total

DIRECTIONS Read and answer each question.

1. Circle the words that need capital letters.

when may i eat my cupcake?

2. Add punctuation.

Math is my favorite subject

3. Write the verb.

The lion _____ for food.
(hunts or cat)

4. Which word is spelled correctly?

bus

buss

 #51172—180 Days of Language

NAME: _____

DIRECTIONS Read and answer each question.

1. Circle the words that need capital letters.

have i ever been on a plane?

1. Ⓨ Ⓝ

2. Add punctuation.

2. Ⓨ Ⓝ

What is school like

3. Ⓨ Ⓝ

3. Circle the noun.

The bag is pink.

4. Ⓨ Ⓝ

___ / 4
Total

4. Which word is spelled correctly?

home

howm

NAME: _____

SCORE

1. Ⓨ Ⓝ

2. Ⓨ Ⓝ

3. Ⓨ Ⓝ

4. Ⓨ Ⓝ

___/ 4
Total

DIRECTIONS Read and answer each question.

1. Circle the words that need capital letters.

can i win this game?

2. Add punctuation.

Is today Monday or Tuesday

3. Circle the verb.

The cat drinks its milk.

4. Which word is spelled correctly?

knee

nee

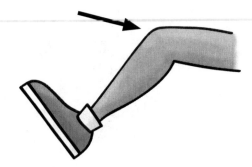

NAME: _____

DIRECTIONS Read and answer each question.

1. Circle the words that need capital letters.

can i play with you?

2. Add punctuation.

The fly buzzed

3. Circle the verb.

The tall man walks away.

4. Which word is spelled correctly?

bugg

bug

SCORE

1. Ⓨ Ⓝ

2. Ⓨ Ⓝ

3. Ⓨ Ⓝ

4. Ⓨ Ⓝ

___ / 4
Total

NAME: _____

DIRECTIONS Read and answer each question.

SCORE

1. Ⓨ Ⓝ

2. Ⓨ Ⓝ

3. Ⓨ Ⓝ

4. Ⓨ Ⓝ

___ / 4
Total

1. Circle the words that need capital letters.

have i seen this show?

2. Add punctuation.

Where is my pet

3. Write the noun.

The _____ is warm today.
(**hop** or **room**)

4. Which word is spelled correctly?

pink

pnk

NAME: _____

DIRECTIONS Read and answer each question.

1. Circle the words that need capital letters.

will i see you today?

2. Add punctuation.

I have never been this happy

3. Write the verb.

Nan _____ every day.
        (**walks** or **paper**)

4. Which word is spelled correctly?

bund

band

NAME: _____

1. Ⓨ Ⓝ

2. Ⓨ Ⓝ

3. Ⓨ Ⓝ

4. Ⓨ Ⓝ

___/4
Total

DIRECTIONS Read and answer each question.

1. Circle the word that needs a capital letter.

May i have another cookie?

2. Add punctuation.

Where did Cole go

3. Write the noun.

The _____ writes a book.
(**talk** or **boy**)

4. Which word is spelled correctly?

lyonn

lion

NAME: _____

DIRECTIONS Read and answer each question.

1. Circle the words that need capital letters.

do i know the way home?

1. Ⓨ Ⓝ

2. Ⓨ Ⓝ

2. Add punctuation.

Let's go home now

3. Ⓨ Ⓝ

4. Ⓨ Ⓝ

3. Circle the nouns.

The glue was in a jar.

___ / 4
Total

4. Which word is spelled correctly?

pyn

pin

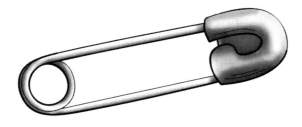

NAME: _____

DIRECTIONS Read and answer each question.

1. Circle the word that needs a capital letter.

i have a messy room.

2. Add punctuation.

Who would do that

3. Circle the verb.

Anna likes worms.

4. Which word is spelled correctly?

culd

cold

NAME: _____

DIRECTIONS Read and answer each question.

1. Circle the words that need capital letters.

jack and i want to play.

1. Ⓨ Ⓝ

2. Ⓨ Ⓝ

2. Add punctuation.

I am very scared

3. Ⓨ Ⓝ

4. Ⓨ Ⓝ

3. Write the noun.

___ / 4
Total

The _____ was inside.

_____

(**goat** or **sad**)

4. Which word is spelled correctly?

hen

henn

NAME: _____

SCORE

1. Ⓨ Ⓝ

2. Ⓨ Ⓝ

3. Ⓨ Ⓝ

4. Ⓨ Ⓝ

___ / 4
Total

1. Which are always capitalized?

months   verbs   nouns

2. Add punctuation.

That movie made me cry a lot

3. Circle the verb.

Jack wears blue pants.

4. Which word is spelled correctly?

loc

lock

NAME: _____

DIRECTIONS Read and answer each question.

1. Which words are always capitalized?

holidays   verbs   nouns

2. Add punctuation.

We worked hard to win the game

3. Write the verb.

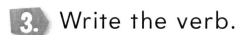

I _____ a bee.

(**hat** or **see**)

4. Which word is spelled correctly?

from   frome

ANSWER KEY

Note: Depending on how students read the sentences that ask for ending punctuation, you may have some students who put periods and some that put exclamation points. Teachers should grade student responses at their discretion.

Day 1
1. **The** dog is fast.
2. The bed is red**.**
3. The pig **runs**.
4. do**g**

Day 2
1. **A** pan is hot.
2. A boy is in the car**.**
3. cats
4. le**g**

Day 3
1. **We** go to bed.
2. Is that a pet**?**
3. The **boy** digs.
4. ba**t**

Day 4
1. **She** is my mom.
2. Why did you go**?**
3. hats
4. ra**t**

Day 5
1. **Who** is home?
2. The jet is loud**!** (or **.**)
3. toes
4. to**y**

Day 6
1. **The** cat is fat.
2. The cat is sad**.**
3. moms
4. he**n**

Day 7
1. **A** rat is wet.
2. When do we go**?**
3. The top **spins**.
4. mu**d**

Day 8
1. **The** boy is sad.
2. I am very sad**!**
3. lids
4. bu**g**

Day 9
1. **Will** the bug run?
2. I love to read**!**
3. The boy **hugs** me.
4. ca**p**

Day 10
1. **Can** you go?
2. I will eat now**.**
3. The cat **hops**.
4. po**t**

Day 11
1. **Can** I go?
2. The tent is wet**.**
3. mops
4. ca**t**

Day 12
1. **Do** you hop?
2. Who will win**?**
3. The bug **ran**.
4. pe**n**

Day 13
1. **Will** I be late?
2. She is very happy**!**
3. The **pot** is hot.
4. **n**ut

Day 14
1. **A** dad can jog.
2. I have a cut**.**
3. The **lamp** is red.
4. ha**t**

Day 15
1. **Can** I see?
2. Max is ten**.**
3. The dog **runs**.
4. si**x**

Day 16
1. **I** have a dog.
2. I like the pink cap**.**
3. Mom **led** me home.
4. lo**g**

Day 17
1. **My** cat is black.
2. That bump is big**.**
3. Can you **jog**?
4. ve**t**

Day 18
1. **I** can run.
2. Who can mop**?**
3. She wants a **toy**.
4. mo**p**

Day 19
1. **Did** you go, too?
2. Will you get me**?**
3. pins
4. te**n**

Day 20
1. The dog and **I** will run.
2. The pot is very hot**!**
3. mats
4. fi**n**

Day 21
1. **I** have a cut.
2. Where do we go**?**
3. The **sock** is red.
4. da**d**

Day 22
1. **The** mom ran.
2. When is it over**?**
3. My **hair** is wet.
4. pe**t**

Day 23
1. **A** cow can sit.
2. I did that for you**.**
3. The **dog** sat on the rug.
4. di**g**

Day 24
1. **Will** he go, too?
2. The run is not fun**.**
3. Jack **hops** on his foot.
4. **r**ug

ANSWER KEY *(cont.)*

Day 25
1. **Do** you see it?
2. The pen is blue**.**
3. Anna **runs** away.
4. h**u**t

Day 26
1. **Can** I fit?
2. The lamp is off**.**
3. The **boy** runs to me.
4. **m**ug

Day 27
1. **Is** that a bad way to go?
2. The nest is on the tree**.**
3. The baby **naps**.
4. c**u**p

Day 28
1. **It** is a big rig.
2. Who can help me**?**
3. The **man** can tap.
4. c**u**t

Day 29
1. **The** jug is pink.
2. Will you rest**?**
3. The **cap** is on his head.
4. p**a**n

Day 30
1. **An** apple is red.
2. That car is fast**!**
3. Mom will **fix** it.
4. **b**us

Day 31
1. **A** dog rests.
2. The vest is wet**.**
3. The **rose** is pink.
4. s**a**d

Day 32
1. **The** sand is hot.
2. Is that a big sink**?**
3. The **lion** is fast.
4. j**u**g

Day 33
1. **Can** you go fast?
2. You are the best mom**!**
3. I see a wet **floor**.
4. n**a**p

Day 34
1. **You** must go run.
2. Where is the milk**?**
3. The nest **sits** on the tree.
4. h**o**p

Day 35
1. **Do** you need a bank?
2. Do we need a tent**?**
3. The **desk** is full.
4. m**oo**n

Day 36
1. **Do** I need a cast?
2. That kid is fast**!**
3. I see a **car**.
4. l**o**g

Day 37
1. **Can** you use the sink?
2. The pump is slow**.**
3. The **cat** rests.
4. j**o**g

Day 38
1 Am **I** the last one?
2. Where will I send it**?**
3. She **moves** the desk.
4. h**o**t

Day 39
1. **Do** you wink?
2. The list is long**.**
3. The man **helps** me.
4. h**u**g

Day 40
1. **It** will be fun.
2. Where are Mom and Dad**?**
3. The crab **walks**.
4. w**i**n or w**o**n

Day 41
1. **I** see the cat.
2. Can I rest**?**
3. The **car** went fast.
4. j**a**r

Day 42
1. **We** can play in the sand.
2. The car went by**.**
3. The **ants** are red.
4. m**o**m

Day 43
1. Will **I** see my dad?
2. I must go now**!** (or **.**)
3. **Sam** sees a **frog**.
4. s**u**n

Day 44
1. **It** is time for milk.
2. The dog is fast**!**
3. The **bumps** are big.
4. p**i**n

Day 45
1. Can **I** go with you?
2. I have cake to eat**.**
3. My **vests** are best.
4. b**i**g

Day 46
1. **I** eat food.
2. Where is the bank**?**
3. Anna **rides** a bike.
4. s**a**nd

Day 47
1. **The** flag is big.
2. The bee is mad**!**
3. **Max** has a pen.
4. dr**i**p or dr**o**p

Day 48
1. **I** see colors.
2. I need to go last**.**
3. Tim **grabs** the paper.
4. m**i**lk

Day 49
1. **The** boy is six.
2. Do you see my hand**?**
3. Ray **has** a car.
4. **m**ask

Day 50
1. **I** need a nap.
2. Do not yell**!** (or **.**)
3. Bea **holds** her doll.
4. **d**rum

Day 51
1. **The** book is short.
2. Do you like bugs**?**
3. My **dad** has a **car**.
4. han**d**

ANSWER KEY (cont.)

Day 52
1. **Let** me go home.
2. My dad is going home**.**
3. Our dog **plays**.
4. **c**rab

Day 53
1. **How** can this be?
2. I am so happy now**!**
3. Books **are** fun.
4. sl**e**d

Day 54
1. **I** saw a bird today.
2. The park was a lot of fun**!**
3. I like **apples**.
4. sin**k**

Day 55
1. **The** play is very long.
2. Today is Monday**.**
3. I **ride** a bike.
4. te**n**t

Day 56
1. **Do** you like to read?
2. Can I go**?**
3. I **see** a tree.
4. flag

Day 57
1. **The** bat is black.
2. I need a new hat**.**
3. I want a **hat**.
4. s**w**im

Day 58
1. **How** do we get home?
2. When is school over**?**
3. I **go** to the park.
4. nest

Day 59
1. **Can** I go with you?
2. How are you doing**?**
3. We eat **apples**.
4. lam**p**

Day 60
1. **A** cat is on the mat.
2. I am very happy**!**
3. I **go** to school.
4. pi**g**

Day 61
1. **I** will send it to you.
2. I like pizza a lot**!**
3. The **crabs** are slow.
4. ram**p**

Day 62
1. **My** list is very long.
2. Where is my hat**?**
3. The **bumps** are big.
4. **b**oy

Day 63
1. **I** need some help!
2. That really hurt**!**
3. The **nests** are full.
4. **p**ond

Day 64
1. **Do** you want to swim?
2. My bike is red**.**
3. Do you wear **masks**?
4. list

Day 65
1. **The** car must stop.
2. The water is very cold**!**
3. You have two **cats**.
4. bum**p**

Day 66
1. May **I** have cake?
2. The tent is big**.**
3. You roll three **balls**.
4. fork

Day 67
1. When will **I** go?
2. What is a hint**?**
3. You have two **cakes**.
4. dra**g**

Day 68
1. **I** play with others.
2. The van is very fast**!**
3. You have four **games**.
4. jet

Day 69
1. **I** read books.
2. Do you have a list**?**
3. You have six **rakes**.
4. star

Day 70
1. **I** can climb.
2. The slug cannot move**.**
3. You have two **dimes**.
4. bend

Day 71
1. **What** is the time?
2. The tide is low**.**
3. The **bird** goes by.
4. bo**x**

Day 72
1. **A** kite flies by.
2. How far is a mile**?**
3. Pat **read** the book.
4. ho**g**

Day 73
1. **The** car is mine.
2. Where is the hole**?**
3. Sam **went** to his home.
4. cop

Day 74
1. **A** mile is far.
2. That dog is very cute**!**
3. The **park** was fun.
4. van

Day 75
1. **The** mice are fun.
2. What is your hope**?**
3. Anna **eats** the pizza.
4. ant

Day 76
1. **I** hope you can come.
2. Today is a good day**.**
3. You have two **rules**.
4. fish

Day 77
1. **Kit** is my friend.
2. The sale is over**.**
3. There are two **bugs**.
4. key

Day 78
1. **The** game is over.
2. Do you have a rope**?**
3. There are two **cages**.
4. rats

 #51172—180 Days of Language

ANSWER KEY *(cont.)*

Day 79
1. **A** lake can be cold.
2. When is June**?**
3. She has two **capes**.
4. d**o**t

Day 80
1. **Please** call me.
2. That is very rude**!**
3. She needs two **dimes**.
4. f**a**n

Day 81
1. **Please** come home.
2. The flag is red**.**
3. The **man** had the **ball**.
4. be**l**t

Day 82
1. **Look** at that crab!
2. Can you play with a ball**?**
3. A **bus** is on the **road**.
4. a**r**m

Day 83
1. **She** likes music.
2. The game was hard**.**
3. Where did the **bird** land on the **nest**?
4. h**o**se

Day 84
1. **Here** is a bulb.
2. Today is a cold day**.**
3. A **cat** has a **toy**.
4. c**a**ve

Day 85
1. **Have** you ever done that?
2. I like apples**.**
3. The **van** had four **tires**.
4. ca**p**e

Day 86
1. **Look** at my hand.
2. The dog loves to walk**.**
3. Val **sees** a rose.
4. ba**ll**

Day 87
1. **My** dad is tall.
2. That is way too loud**!**
3. Eve **likes** movies.
4. ro**b**e

Day 88
1. **Go** to school today.
2. Who likes to play ball**?**
3. Ned **needs** his book.
4. co**n**e

Day 89
1. **Do** you have the time?
2. I do not know his name**.**
3. Min **said** yes.
4. lea**f**

Day 90
1. **Why** are you sad?
2. The apple is red**.**
3. The dog **barks**.
4. ga**t**e

Day 91
1. Answers will vary.
2. I like to swim**.**
3. **He** cut the paper.
4. b**o**ne

Day 92
1. **I** am 5 years old.
2. Can I go**?**
3. Rob **ate** his food.
4. ca**r**

Day 93
1. Answers will vary.
2. That was a great game**!**
3. The **cat** is very fast.
4. bi**r**d

Day 94
1. Answers will vary.
2. When is lunch**?**
3. The **car** is pink.
4. ra**c**e

Day 95
1. **How** are you?
2. I want to hop**.**
3. The cat **ran** away.
4. hi**d**e

Day 96
1. "**Look** at me," **I** said.
2. Where is the spot**?**
3. The vet **works** hard.
4. b**e**e

Day 97
1. "**This** is fun," I said.
2. Where will you go**?**
3. My mom **walks** fast.
4. c**a**t

Day 98
1. **When** do **I** get to go?
2. I am very happy to see you**!**
3. **Miss Kane** is my **teacher**.
4. fro**g**

Day 99
1. **I** said that **I** will help.
2. I ate rice and beans**.**
3. The jay **sits** in the nest.
4. sl**u**g

Day 100
1. Can **I** get over the bump?
2. Watch out for the car**!**
3. **Hal** has a **book**.
4. doo**r**

Day 101
1. **This** is the first page.
2. Where is my mom**?**
3. **Jan** likes the **movie**.
4. ba**th**

Day 102
1. **A** cap is on my head.
2. The crab moves**.**
3. Kim **goes** to her room.
4. si**d**e

ANSWER KEY *(cont.)*

Day 103
1. **Will** I see you?
2. The pig has to eat**.**
3. **Fred** has a **bag**.
4. fish

Day 104
1. **She** can do it.
2. That is too fast**!**
3. **Evan** likes to play **soccer**.
4. lion

Day 105
1. **He** may be mad.
2. Who can help me**?**
3. **Nan** has a **baby**.
4. dish

Day 106
1. **The** ice is cold.
2. When will school start**?**
3. **Ava** went to **bed**.
4. sing

Day 107
1. **Put** the dog in his cage.
2. The bunny went away**.**
3. **Pam** needs a **lunch**.
4. cow

Day 108
1. **I** love you very much!
2. Why do you need the hat**?**
3. The **coin** is shiny.
4. wor**m**

Day 109
1. **Will** you play with me?
2. The band is loud**!**
3. **Jane** was so kind.
4. eye

Day 110
1. **The** corn was good!
2. The plant is tall**.**
3. The **train** went by the **road**.
4. face

Day 111
1. **A** deer came over to me.
2. Kate was very mad**!**
3. The **car** sped by.
4. jeep

Day 112
1. **The** mice were gray.
2. Why was the tire flat**?**
3. The **dog** plays.
4. wave

Day 113
1. **Can** you help me?
2. Is that a rose**?**
3. The **creek** is cold.
4. seat

Day 114
1. **Will** you hold it?
2. I hope it is true**.**
3. My feet **tap**.
4. bi**k**e

Day 115
1. **My** dog is slow.
2. Does the cat bite**?**
3. The ice cream **drips**.
4. rose

Day 116
1. Do **I** need to say it?
2. Jay sees a bug**.**
3. Lee **plans** his work.
4. meal

Day 117
1. **How** will **I** know?
2. Sam needs a hug**.**
3. Jake **runs** away.
4. kite

Day 118
1. May **I** have that?
2. Who is in the car**?**
3. The ice cube **melts**.
4. fold

Day 119
1. **I** think she is nice.
2. Watch out**!**
3. Dave **walks** to his car.
4. mow

Day 120
1. **I** see the new rug.
2. I miss you**!** (or .)
3. Nate **sees** a bird.
4. nail

Day 121
1. **I** need help.
2. Do you want a red one**?**
3. Jim **feels** happy.
4. coin

Day 122
1. **We** can bake a pie.
2. Do you need a tack**?**
3. The cat can **jump**.
4. bed

Day 123
1. **My** mom is not home.
2. I am very mad**.** (or !)
3. The girl **reads** the book.
4. wi**n**k

Day 124
1. **Max** is kind to me.
2. Why are you sad**?**
3. **Rick** walks to **school**.
4. **b**ee

Day 125
1. **I** hope to see the doll.
2. Do not go home**!** (or .)
3. My mom **gave** me a gift.
4. rock

Day 126
1. **Sam** is my friend.
2. How will I get that done**?**
3. The **home** is on a **street**.
4. duck

Day 127
1. Do **I** need to be here?
2. That is very scary**!**
3. I **wrote** a code.
4. clock

Day 128
1. **Can I** have that?
2. The cat is lazy**.**
3. The **plant** grows tall.
4. ring

Day 129
1. **My** pal is at home.
2. The robe is on a hook**.**
3. I **rode** in the car.
4. bell

ANSWER KEY (cont.)

Day 130
1. **Jill** wants to go to school.
2. Where is my note**?**
3. She will **dine** now.
4. p**a**ck

Day 131
1. **My** mop is in the pail.
2. Who will come over and play**?**
3. The **baby** is sad.
4. f**o**x

Day 132
1. **The** tent is full of dust.
2. I am very happy with you**!**
3. Jan **hides** from me.
4. sn**ai**l

Day 133
1. **Will** you send it to me?
2. I will use the hose**.**
3. Dan **hikes** up the hill.
4. s**e**al

Day 134
1. **When** can we swim?
2. Do we go in June**?**
3. Hank **rides** to work.
4. tu**be**

Day 135
1. **Do** you need help?
2. What is that tune**?**
3. June **piles** the paper.
4. w**e**b

Day 136
1. **How** do I make that?
2. Do not let go of the rope**!**
3. He has three **bones**.
4. m**o**p

Day 137
1. **I** want to pick a rose.
2. Fly the kite for me**.**
3. I see six **tiles**.
4. r**i**nk

Day 138
1. **Take** the book to bed.
2. I want to bake a cake**.**
3. I have five pine **cones**.
4. t**u**b

Day 139
1. **Do** not poke me!
2. The race is over**.**
3. Let's play ten **games**.
4. b**i**b

Day 140
1. **I** woke up at six.
2. Jake got in the car**.**
3. I can see four **races**.
4. wago**n**

Day 141
1. **I** can hear the tune.
2. Is it Monday**?**
3. I see five **lakes**.
4. **m**ap

Day 142
1. **The** bell will ring.
2. I pet the dog**.**
3. There are ten **waves**.
4. **m**ice

Day 143
1. **That** sure looks good.
2. I am very happy**!**
3. I have six **dimes**.
4. lime

Day 144
1. **Can** Hal play?
2. I want pizza**.**
3. I took six **bites**.
4. **m**ail

Day 145
1. **Is** the dog black or brown?
2. Is it raining**?**
3. The **poles** are tall.
4. **n**ose

Day 146
1. **Do** you want some cake?
2. The hive was buzzing**.**
3. The kitten **sat** in the yard.
4. cat

Day 147
1. **Jack** is a good friend.
2. Does this work**?**
3. The girl **hugs** the doll.
4. hit

Day 148
1. **That** was a hot day!
2. The beach was too cold**!**
3. The **team** works hard.
4. top

Day 149
1. **Ned** does not like to lose.
2. How can we get home**?**
3. The hare **runs** fast.
4. mom

Day 150
1. **Fran** does not like bikes.
2. This is the best day ever**!**
3. **She** took care of me.
4. rat

Day 151
1. **The** bird is in the sky.
2. Who is your teacher**?**
3. The **man** likes the **book**.
4. rake

Day 152
1. **An** apple is good to eat.
2. Look at that car zoom by**!**
3. Ken **asked** to his friend over.
4. clip

Day 153
1. **One** day, I will go there.
2. Where is your house**?**
3. The **boy** works hard.
4. drip

ANSWER KEY *(cont.)*

Day 154
1. **Some** kids are nice.
2. The story was too short.
3. A **toy** is fun to play with.
4. shop

Day 155
1. **Next** time, I will go first.
2. I want to go home right now!
3. The **boat** came to **shore**.
4. frog

Day 156
1. **After** dinner, I sleep.
2. Are you going home?
3. Rick loves to **play**.
4. snap

Day 157
1. **Thank** you for my gift.
2. May feels very sad!
3. My dad washed my **dog**.
4. drum

Day 158
1. **May** I help you?
2. When is the party?
3. The **man** helps the class.
4. bike

Day 159
1. **Put** the book down.
2. She will clean her room.
3. My mom **gives** hugs.
4. bird

Day 160
1. **Stop** being so loud!
2. Can I play with your toys?
3. Maria hugs her **cat**.
4. play

Day 161
1. **When** can **I** go home?
2. I like to drink milk.
3. She needs three **limes**.
4. slow

Day 162
1. **Do I** need to run today?
2. I need to take a rest.
3. I love my **pets**.
4. hop

Day 163
1. **Will** I ever find out the secret?
2. May I have more time?
3. Evan read four **books**.
4. stop

Day 164
1. May **I** go to the store with you?
2. What is your name?
3. I want two **bikes**.
4. bell

Day 165
1. **Who** can **I** help today?
2. I ate my lunch.
3. There are three **desks**.
4. book

Day 166
1. **When** do **I** go to sleep?
2. Who will be on my team?
3. I **skip** to school.
4. boy

Day 167
1. **How** can **I** do that?
2. I really love to go to the beach!
3. Birds **fly** in the sky.
4. cap

Day 168
1. **Do I** need to get shots today?
2. Can we have pizza every day?
3. **He** is on a bike.
4. food

Day 169
1. **When** may **I** eat my cupcake?
2. Math is my favorite subject.
3. The lion **hunts** for food.
4. bus

Day 170
1. **Have I** ever been on a plane?
2. What is school like?
3. The **bag** is pink.
4. home

Day 171
1. **Can I** win this game?
2. Is today Monday or Tuesday?
3. The cat **drinks** its milk.
4. knee

Day 172
1. **Can I** play with you?
2. The fly buzzed.
3. The tall man **walks** away.
4. bug

Day 173
1. **Have I** seen this show?
2. Where is my pet?
3. The **room** is warm today.
4. pink

Day 174
1. **Will I** see you today?
2. I have never been this happy!
3. Nan **walks** every day.
4. band

Day 175
1. May **I** have another cookie?
2. Where did Cole go?
3. The **boy** writes a book.
4. lion

Day 176
1. **Do I** know the way home?
2. Let's go home now! (or .)
3. The **glue** was in a **jar**.
4. pin

ANSWER KEY *(cont.)*

Day 177
1. **I** have a messy room.
2. Who would do that**?**
3. Anna **likes** worms.
4. cold

Day 178
1. **Jack** and **I** want to play.
2. I am very scared**!**
3. The **goat** was inside.
4. hen

Day 179
1. months
2. That movie made me cry a lot**!**
3. Jack **wears** blue pants.
4. lock

Day 180
1. holidays
2. We worked hard to win the game**.**
3. I **see** a bee.
4. from

My Language Book

by

_____

- -

_____

#51172—180 Days of Language

Capitalization

Always capitalize the **first word in a sentence**.

Example: The cat ran.

Always capitalize the word *I*.

Example: Do I need to go?

Always capitalize **names of people**.

Example: My friend's name is Kyle.

Always capitalize the **days of the week**.

Example: Today is Monday.

Always capitalize **names of holidays**.

Example: I cannot wait for Earth Day!

Always capitalize **months of the year**.

Example: It rains in June.

Punctuation

Symbol	Definition
. **period**	A **period** means the sentence is finished.
? **question mark**	A **question mark** means the sentence is a question.
! **exclamation point**	An **exclamation point** means there is strong feeling in the sentence.
, **comma**	A **comma** separates words or parts in a sentence.
" " **quotation marks**	**Quotation marks** mean someone is speaking.

Parts of Speech

A **noun** is the name of a person, an animal, a place, or a thing. It is also the subject in a sentence.

Example: The <u>dog</u> ran.

A **plural noun** means there is more than one noun.

Example: The <u>dogs</u> ran.

A **pronoun** takes the place of a noun.

Example: <u>He</u> ran.

A **verb** is the word in a sentence that names an action.

Example: I <u>play</u> at the park.

An **adjective** describes a noun.

Example: <u>The</u> flower is <u>red</u>.

An **adverb** describes a verb or an adjective.

Example 1: He walks <u>slowly</u>.

Example 2: The flower is <u>very</u> red.

Spelling

List 1	List 2	List 3	List 4
the	or	will	number
of	one	up	no
and	had	other	way
a	by	about	could
to	words	out	people
in	but	many	my
is	not	then	than
you	what	them	first
that	all	these	water
it	were	so	been
he	we	some	called
was	when	her	who
for	your	would	oil
on	can	make	sit
are	said	like	now
as	there	him	find
with	use	into	long
his	an	time	down
they	each	has	day
I	which	look	did
at	she	two	get
be	do	more	come
this	how	write	made
have	their	go	may
from	if	see	part

Dr. Fry's 1000 Instant Words ©2004 Teacher Created Materials

Spelling

List 5	List 6	List 7	List 8
over	say	set	try
new	great	put	kind
sound	where	end	hand
take	help	does	picture
only	through	another	again
little	much	well	change
work	before	large	off
know	line	must	play
place	right	big	spell
years	too	even	air
live	means	such	away
me	old	because	animal
back	any	turn	house
give	same	here	point
most	tell	why	page
very	boy	ask	letter
after	follow	went	mother
things	came	men	answer
our	want	read	found
just	show	need	study
name	also	land	still
good	around	different	learn
sentence	form	home	should
man	three	us	America
think	small	move	world

Dr. Fry's 1000 Instant Words ©2004 Teacher Created Materials

Spelling

List 5	List 6	List 7	List 8
high	saw	important	miss
every	left	until	idea
near	don't	children	enough
add	few	side	eat
food	while	feet	face
between	along	car	watch
own	might	mile	far
below	close	night	Indian
country	something	walk	real
plant	seem	white	almost
last	next	sea	let
school	hard	began	above
father	open	grow	girl
keep	example	took	sometimes
tree	begin	river	mountains
never	life	four	cut
start	always	carry	young
cry	those	state	talk
earth	both	once	soon
eyes	paper	book	list
light	together	hear	song
thought	got	stop	being
head	group	without	leave
under	often	second	family
story	run	late	it's

Dr. Fry's 1000 Instant Words ©2004 Teacher Created Materials

REFERENCES CITED

Haussamen, Brock. 2014. "Some Questions and Answers About Grammar." Retrieved from http://www.ateg.org/grammar/qna.php.

Hillocks, George, Jr., and Michael W. Smith. 1991. "Grammar and Usage." In *Handbook of Research on Teaching the English Language Arts*. James Flood, Julie M. Jensen, Diane Lapp, and James R. Squire. New York: Macmillan.

Hodges, Richard E. 1991. "The Conventions of Writing." In *Handbook of Research on Teaching the English Language Arts*. James Flood, Julie M. Jensen, Diane Lapp, and James R. Squire. New York: Macmillan.

———. 2003. "Grammar and Literacy Learning." In *Handbook of Research on Teaching the English Language Arts*, 2nd ed. James Flood, Julie M. Jensen, Diane Lapp, and James R. Squire. New York: Macmillan.

Lederer, Richard. 1987. *Anguished English: An Anthology of Accidental Assaults upon Our Language.* New York: Dell.

Marzano, Robert J. 2010. When Practice Makes Perfect. . .Sense. *Educational Leadership* 68(3): 81–83.

Truss, Lynne. 2003. *Eats, Shoots and Leaves: The Zero Tolerance Approach to Punctuation.* New York: Gotham Books.

CONTENTS OF THE DIGITAL RESOURCE CD

Teacher Resources

Resource	Filename
Diagnostic Assessment Directions	directions.pdf
Practice Page Item Analysis	pageitem.pdf pageitem.doc pageitem.xls
Student Item Analysis	studentitem.pdf studentitem.doc studentitem.xls
Standards Chart	standards.pdf

Student Resources

All of the 180 practice pages are contained in a single PDF. In order to print specific days, open the PDF and select the pages to print.

Resource	Filename
Practice Pages Day 1–Day 180	practicepages.pdf
My Language Book	languagebook.pdf